# AMERICAN EDUCATION

*Its Men*

*Ideas*

*and*

*Institutions*

Advisory Editor

*Lawrence A. Cremin*
Frederick A. P. Barnard Professor of Education
Teachers College, Columbia University

# The Development
# of School Support
# in Colonial Massachusetts

George Leroy Jackson

ARNO PRESS & THE NEW YORK TIMES
*New York * 1969*

Reprint edition 1969 by Arno Press, Inc.

*

Library of Congress Catalog Card No. 75-89190

*

Reprinted from a copy in The Free Public Library of Newark

*

Manufactured in the United States of America

# Editorial Note

AMERICAN EDUCATION: *Its Men, Institutions and Ideas*
presents selected works of thought and scholarship that have
long been out of print or otherwise unavailable. Inevitably, such
works will include particular ideas and doctrines that have been
outmoded or superseded by more recent research. Nevertheless,
all retain their place in the literature, having influenced educational thought and practice in their own time and having provided
the basis for subsequent scholarship.

*Lawrence A. Cremin*
Teachers College

# The Development
## of School Support
## in Colonial Massachusetts

# THE DEVELOPMENT OF SCHOOL SUPPORT IN COLONIAL MASSACHUSETTS

BY

George Leroy Jackson, Ph. D.

TEACHERS COLLEGE, COLUMBIA UNIVERSITY
CONTRIBUTIONS TO EDUCATION, NO. 25

PUBLISHED BY
Teachers College, Columbia University
NEW YORK CITY
1909

PRESS OF
BRANDOW PRINTING COMPANY
ALBANY, N. Y.

# CONTENTS

## CHAPTER I

### INTRODUCTION

## CHAPTER II

### SCHOOL SUPPORT BY CONTRIBUTION

## CHAPTER III

### FREE EDUCATION FOR THE POOR

## CHAPTER IV

### RECORDS OF TOWN ACTION WITH RESPECT TO SCHOOL SUPPORT

## CHAPTER V

### SCHOOL SUPPORT BY GENERAL TAXATION

## CHAPTER VI

### THE " FREE SCHOOL "

# CHAPTER I

## INTRODUCTION

The aim of this study is, first, to trace the various methods through which the early schools of Massachusetts were supported—showing at the same time the basis of experience for dealing with the problem of support through the close relationship existing between—1) education and religion, and 2) education and the support and apprenticeship of the poor; and, second, after partial support by general taxation had become customary, to point out the main causes which made general taxation the *sole* method of school support and hence gave rise to the " free school "—publicly controlled and publicly supported.

The men who managed affairs in the early Massachusetts towns were beyond question influenced by the methods and ideals which prevailed in the mother country. We know that in England there was a close relationship in Puritan thought between education and religion, hence there would be a definite tendency to continue the same relationship in the colony. The mere incident of a sea-voyage would scarcely destroy all associations formed up to that time. We know that for years the English people had been working out the problem of poor relief and during the life of the colonists in England had arrived at a definite method of caring for the poor, hence it is highly improbable that, when the necessity arose, this method should not occur to the colonists as a possible way of solving a similar difficulty. In other words there can be no doubt that what these men had thought and done in England was the basis of their thinking and doing in the Massachusetts Colony. Hence in meeting the practical problem of supporting any institution we would expect them to use the prevailing English method, or a modification of that method, or the application for the support of one institution of the prevailing or modified English method of supporting another.

In the matter of school support, as we shall see later, the English methods were not suited to the social and economic conditions of the early colony. Some other method had to be found and we know that the present method, general taxation, was not the first. Under these circumstances we would expect

the early solution of the problem to be influenced by the methods
used in meeting other charges of a public nature, especially by
the methods used in supporting those public charges closely connected with the school. For this reason it has seemed best, since
the records with respect to the early schools are so few, to show
the development of church and poor support in the Colony. If
we find distinct methods of meeting the charges incident to the
maintenance of the church, and of the poor—including the apprenticeship of poor children—and if here and there we find a
record showing that a school was maintained through a similar
method, we have as conclusive proof as may be of the method
or methods through which schools were maintained during the
early period. Expressed in somewhat graphic form by representing well defined methods by heavy lines and the less well defined
by dots the general argument from relationship and suggestion
is as indicated:

———— ———— ——— support of poor in England.
———— ———— ——— support of the church in Mass.
· · · — · · — ——— support of the school in Mass.

It is essential by way of introduction to our study to make a
more detailed analysis of those phases of experience which are
pertinent to the furtherance of its aim; (1) to enquire somewhat
into the ideals which were fundamental to the Puritan religion
and the relation of such ideals to the necessity of education; (2)
to enquire into the methods of poor support in England since
for centuries there had been a close relationship between the
church, the poor, and the education of youth; (3) to state a
few pertinent facts with respect to civil and social conditions in
the early settlements. These topics form no part of our investi-
gation but serve to put us in touch with the general conditions
necessary to give the social and historical setting of the problem.

1. The fundamental principle of the Renaissance and its northern aspect, the Reformation, was the firm conviction that liberty
and reason lay at the basis of individuality and that individual
achievement was most worth while. In the South, a civilization
of pagan origin which during the pagan period produced some
of the world's best thoughts and artistic products naturally turned
to those great masterpieces for uplift and guidance; in the North,
a people who before Christianity had produced nothing, by the

same natural process turned to the Bible and the patristic writings, the sources from which the Northern civilization had sprung. In either case it was the Era of the New Learning, an eager searching after Truth in the manuscript and the printed page and, in the North especially, a dependence upon the authority of the Bible which was as great as had been the previous sway of Aristotle. But though the Scriptures were the great authority the spirit of the Reformation demanded that this authority be individually declared—not by priest or pope to the unthinking and receptive masses but by the best interpretation of its commands and precepts which the individual might be able to make for himself. Liberty and reason were the basis for a new relationship between God and man.

This startling innovation in method of thought and action was soon modified. It was too anarchistic to allow men to live together in any degree of harmony; too opposed to the natural instinct to form like-minded groups. And so, consciously or unconsciously, men took from the Bible that which best suited their ideas and dispositions—creeds began to fetter the free exercise of thought and narrowness and intolerance were rampant. Learning became narrower in scope and purpose, yet learning was necessary to compass even this faint remnant of the Reformation ideal. Whatever remained of liberty and reason seems to have been transferred from the individual to the group and it fought as valiantly and persistently for its as did ever Luther for his tenets.

The point here to be emphasized is, that however false men have proved to be at times to the Reformation ideal it has always demanded at its best an enlightened people and an educated clergy. The Bible was put into the hands of the people to be for each one an individual guide and help and at least an education sufficient to read and understand it was a necessary corollary. That such was the case is evidenced by the school systems established in Saxony, Wurtenberg, Gotha and other German States under the influence of the Reformation movement. The root idea being to give reading, writing, and singing to all, with higher schools to act as selective agents for the State and ministry. By means of education Erasmus, Luther, Melanchthon, Duke Ernest and many others hoped to reform well nigh unendurable conditions and raise the general moral plane of mankind to a higher level through educated leadership of a reading, thinking people.

It was against dogmatism, authority, form, pretence that Puritanism and its sister movements Pietism and Jansenism arose. Conduct, faith, piety, righteousness, and good works, the holding up of high individual standards marked this movement and made its followers stand out distinctly. The religious tenets of the Puritans believed to have been ably and faithfully worked out of the Scriptures, at first carried out the best traditions of the Reformation in the general ideas expressed above; that they soon became narrow and intolerant is but the fault of the age. The fact that they believed themselves to be God's elect as proved by the Bible, that their way of thinking and doing must therefore be the only possible escape from punishment and the way whereby mankind might be saved made them the stronger and more persistent in their ideas when they were met by opposition and persecution. The Puritan was one with the Reformation in his belief in his power to draw inspiration from God, to have direct personal communion between each human being and his Maker, and to find in the Bible, each man for himself, the guiding principles of all his thoughts and acts.

Nothing could be stronger than the Puritan belief in the Bible. The Westminster Confession which the Puritan accepted teaches that all things necessary for man's salvation are found in the Scriptures; that they were immediately inspired by God and contain within themselves the infallible rule of interpretation; and that they commanded all the people of God to read and search them.[1] Unquestionably the Bible and the capacity to read it was an essential part of Puritan society derived from the general Reformation movement. They did not wish a blind acceptance of their faith but that each should read for himself and embrace the Creed through conviction of the righteousness of their faith. Such conviction was possible only to those who could read a Bible whose authenticity was vouched for by a still higher scholarship. They were God's elect, but to deserve His protection each one must read, ponder over the Scriptures and the explanation by the minister in order to know His will.

---

[1] Westminster Confession, Chap. I., Section VI., VII., IX., VIII.

Unquestionably the spirit of Puritanism demanded that religion and education go hand in hand. The following quotations from De Montmorency's " State Intervention in English Education " bear directly upon this point:

" In 1561 Knox and the early reformers added to the First Book of Discipline certain regulations about schools and colleges, which if they had been carried into effect would have given us before now an almost perfect system of education. Knox proposed that the entire revenues of the old Church should be devoted to the maintenance of schools, of ministers, and of the infirm poor."[2]

Though a little later than the settlement of Massachusetts the Welsh Education Act of 1649 was worked out by men of the same generation and religious faith and hence may be introduced as pertinent to our discussion:

"The Parliament of England taking into their serious consideration the great Duty and Trust that lies on them to use all lawful ways and means for the propagation of the Gospel of Jesus Christ in this Commonwealth, in order thereunto, Do Enact and Ordain, and be it Enacted and Ordained by this present Parliament, and by the Authority thereof, That (..........) are hereby constituted and appointed to be Commissioners in (..........)....That they the said Commissioners or any five or more of them, shall have full power and authority, and are hereby enabled and authorized to receive all articles or charges which shall be exhibited against any Parson, Vicar, Curate, Schoolmaster, or any other now having, or that shall have any Ecclesiastical benefit or promotion within the said counties or any of them......"[3]

It is clear that in the eyes of the Puritan Commonwealth a schoolmastership was regarded as an appointment that ranked with a benefice.

This same Puritan spirit caused the Scottish Parliament in 1633 to empower the Bishop, with the consent of the major part of the tax-payers to enforce a rate on land for the benefit of the school.[4]

All that has been said on this topic is a matter of common knowledge but, as has been previously said, it seems best to bring these points together that we may have a clear conception of the main religious ideas and motives—experience stuff—which was a part of the mental outfit of the New England Puritan. It

---

[2] De Montmorency, State Intervention in English Education, 116–117.
[3] Ibid. 101.
[4] Ibid. 119.

has also seemed legitimate for the purposes of this study to indicate the general results of these same religious ideas and motives as they worked themselves out with reference to church and school in Scotland and Wales. And so before turning to the next topic, the development of the support of the poor in England, let us bring together by way of summary the general aims of the Puritan faith wherever found. Briefly they are: Individual responsibility to God; the Bible the guide to conduct; the ability to read; and the consequent close relationship between religion and education.

2. The last stage in the development of the support of the poor in England—that is, general taxation, was completed during the years of the early colonists' residence in the mother country and was, therefore, a highly pertinent factor in the general mass of experience which might be brought to bear on any question of support. The poor law of England was of importance also from another point of view since its essential features were incorporated in the Massachusetts law of 1642 which made education compulsory for all and formed the basis for free instruction for poor children.

Previous to the confiscation of monastic and guild property by Henry VIII. there had been no legislation with respect to the poor and their support. In the cities, the guilds had taken care of their members when sick or disabled, had pensioned the widows, and paid the apprentice fees of the children; in the country districts the monasteries had played a similar rôle for the support of the poor. With the confiscation of these sources of supply for relief, legislation begins. The first of importance is 5 & 6 Edward VI. cap. 2. It directs the collectors " to gently ask and demand of every man and woman what they of their charity will give weekly towards relief of the poor."

In 5 Elizabeth cap. 3, the following addition seems to have been necessary: " That if any person of his froward or wilful mind shall obstinately refuse to give wekly to the relief of the poor according to his ability " the justices may tax such persons according to their discretion. The method was round-about and not completely given here but it established the principle that property be held subject to the relief of the destitute.

14 Elizabeth, cap. 5 directs the justices to tax the inhabitants and appoint persons to collect the amount levied. This Act

differs from the preceding in that it went direct to its object and provided the requisite machinery for collection and distribution.

Turning now to the apprentice features of the Laws. It was enacted by 27 Henry VIII. cap. 25 that all children between five and thirteen who were begging or in idleness might be appointed to masters in husbandry or other craft. 16 Elizabeth cap. 3 ordered the justices to provide a stock of wood, hemp, flax, iron, and other stuff by taxation in order that poor youth might be trained up in labor and work. 39 Elizabeth cap. 3 gave the overseers of the poor with the consent of two justices the power to " set to work the children of all such whose parents shall not be thought able to keep and maintain them." They were also empowered to raise by taxation an amount sufficient to pay the apprenticeship fees of such children.

All the foregoing laws are summed up in 43 Elizabeth cap. 2 (1601) in which the first section provides that overseers of the poor shall be annually nominated for each parish by the justices. To these are added the churchwardens and from two to four substantial householders according to the size of the parish. Their duty is—

(1) To take measures, with the consent of two justices, for setting to work children whose parents are unable to maintain them;

(2) To raise weekly by taxation of every inhabitant and occupier, such sums as they shall think fit—

(a) For obtaining a convenient stock of flax, hemp, wool, and other necessaries for the poor to work upon;

(b) For putting out poor children as apprentices.

The particular facts which we are to keep in mind with respect to the development of poor support, since they are pertinent to our further discussion, are, that it passed through three definite stages, (1) the period of voluntary contribution, (2) the period of compulsory contribution, and (3) the period of general taxation; that the apprenticeship law was purely industrial in character, that all necessary charges were met by taxation, and that properly constituted authorities had the power to apprentice children and youths; and that this Law of Elizabeth was transferred in all its essential details to the colonial Law of 1642 which made education compulsory for all and free to poor children.

3. The transfer of the government from England to the Colony itself in 1629, coupled with the idea of making New England a refuge for the Puritan believers and a proper place to found a Biblical Commonwealth was the signal for a general movement to the New World. Before Christmas of that year more than 1,000 colonists had landed on the New England coast. The ministers who emigrated were men of standing and influence. Among the laity were many graduates of Cambridge and many who were well versed in public affairs. By far the great majority were men of purpose and character and the influence of these men must always be kept in the foreground in a discussion of the shaping of the early policies of the Colony.

The Company as a trading corporation held title to all the land within its grants and it, through the General Court, granted land to each of the stockholders and larger tracts to a number of individuals in common on condition that they establish a town and a church. These individuals became the proprietors and in turn granted home lots, farms, and rights of common to such applicants as they saw fit to admit to their number. As an example of the origin of a town let us examine the method pursued at Dedham which is typical of any one of the other towns of the Colony.

The first step was a petition to the Court, in which a certain tract of land was mentioned, that the petitioners might "haue and enjoye all those Lands Meadows, Woods and other grounds. together with all the Waters and other benifits what so euer now being or that may be within the Compass of the afore said limits to vs with our ascociates and our assignes for euer."[5]

All newcomers as they were voted into the minor corporation received assignments of land, married men being given home lots of twelve acres; if not married, they were given eight acres each. All such persons were first, however, required to sign the town covenant which shows the spirit of the undertaking so well that it will be given entire:

"1 We whose names ar here vnto subscribed. doe. in the feare and Reuerence of our Allmightie God, Mutually: and seuerally pmise amongst our seules and each to other to pffese and practice one trueth according to that most pfect rule. the foundacion where of is Euerlasting Loue:

"2 That we shall by all meanes Laboure to keepe of from vs all such as ar contrarye minded. And receaue onely such vnto vs as be such

___

[5] Dedham Records, Vol. III., I.

as may be pbably of one harte, with vs as that we either knowe or may well and truely be informed to walke in a peaceable conuersation with all meekness of spirit for the edification of each other in the knowledge and faith of the Lord Jesus: And the mutuall encouragmt vnto all Temporall comforts in all things: seekeing the good of each other out of all which may be deriued true Peace

"3 That if at any time difference shall arise betwene pties of our said Towne. that then such ptie and pties shall prsently Referre all such difference vnto som one. 2 or. 3 others of our said societie to be fully accorded and determined without any firther delaye if it possibly may bee:

"4 That euery man that now, or at any time heereafter shall haue Lotts in our said Towne shall paye his share in all such rates of money and charges as shall be imposed vpon him Rateably on pportion with other men As allso become freely subject vnto all such orders and constitutions as shall be necessariely had or made now or at any time heere after from this daye fore warde as well for Loveing and comfortable societie in our said Towne as allso for the psperous and thriueing Condicion of our said Fellowshipe especially respecting the feare of God in which we desire to begine and continue what so euer we shall by his Loveing fauoure take in hand."[6]

In passing it will be well to notice the main characteristics which mark the settlement of this town—the deeply religious motive, the desire to build up a homogeneous community, the spirit of mutual helpfulness in both spiritual and temporal affairs, and the paying of whatever rates that might be imposed for the well-being of the community. It may be safely held that these motives underlay the founding of all the early New England towns.

At first it was thought that all the business of the "Country" might be transacted by the freemen meeting in a body four times a year but so many applied for the privilege of the franchise that this method was found impossible. The very number applying alarmed the Court and made it fear for the future of the undertaking, therefore it added to the freeman's oath the further qualification:

"To the end the body of the commons may be preserved of honest and good men, it was likewise ordered and agreed, that for the time to come no man shall be admitted to the freedom of the body politic, but such as are members of some of the churches within the limits of the same."[7]

This measure effectually secured the result wished for, namely, that all laws of the Commonwealth be made by men of the Puri-

---

[6] Dedham Records, III. 2–3.
[7] Mass. Col. Rec. I., 87.

tan faith and the Congregational Church since none but freemen of the towns could vote in the election of deputies. So we may be certain that all laws made by the General Court and enforced on all the colonists were in keeping with Puritan ideals.

In the towns, with respect to local affairs, the franchise seems not to have been so restricted and there is every probability that whatever ordinances were passed or rates levied represented the majority opinion of the townsmen and rate-payers, although many were not members of the Church and thus not entitled to the general franchise. In 1647 the right of suffrage was legally extended to the townsmen but in answer to a petition from Ipswich in 1658 the Court held that freemen of the town might restrict such townsmen for cause from exercising this right.[8] This left the directing force in the hands of the freemen as before though I find no evidence of such power having been used.

In a cursory way the following points have been indicated and they are to be especially borne in mind when considering the early period since during that time recorded actions concerning schools are very few: (1) The general intelligence of all the early colonists and the importance to the settlements of the large number of college men who as ministers and leaders were so influential in counseling and guiding new endeavors and policies as well as keeping up the best traditions of English Puritanism; (2) the deep religious and moral convictions fundamental to all their acts; (3) the spirit of co-operation and helpfulness; (4) the general participation of the townsmen in all that pertained to local government, and the consequent adaptation of general policies to local needs and ideas.

Under the three preceding heads we have attempted to give a formulation of well known facts, ideals, and tendencies which entered into the experience and formed the character of the early New England Puritan. All this he brought with him and this mass of experience formed the basis of every working hypothesis which was made toward the solution of new problems of state, church, or school to which the exigencies of a new environment gave rise. Connected experiences of the Old still remained connected in the New World and in the immediate study of the problem, especially during the early period, to which we now turn we are to keep this fact in mind.

---

[8] Mass. Col. Rec. IV., 335.

# CHAPTER II

## School Support by Contribution

We now propose to discuss the relation between religion and education in the early history of the Massachusetts towns in order to form some basis of judgment as to the existence or non-existence of schools during the early period in which the town made few, if any, records of a school; also to take up the methods of church support since, as we shall find that the church and the school are closely affiliated, the development of the one will aid in the explanation of the development of the other. This is especially desirable for during the early period, as we have mentioned above, records concerning the schools are not sufficient in themselves to establish clearly the general methods of support.

Matthew Craddock, the Governor of the Massachusetts Bay Company, in 1629, wrote as follows to John Endicott, the deputy governor of the Colony:

"We are very Confident of yor best endevors for the genrall good, & wee doubt not but God will in mrcye give a blessinge vpon our laboures, & wee trust you will not be vnmindfull of the mayne end of our plantacon by Indevoringe to bringe ye Indians to the knowledge of the gospell; wch yt it maye be speedier & better effected, ye earnest desire of our whole Compa is yt you have dilligent & watchfull Eye on our owne people, that they live unblemished & without reproofe, & demeane themselves justlye & Curteous towards ye Indians, thereby to drawe them to affect our prsons and consequently our religion; as alsoe to endeavore to gett some of theire Children to trayne up to readinge & Consequently to Religion, whilest they are younge."[1]

In the Act of 1642 which dealt with the general educational condition of the Colony, we find that the men chosen to look after the town affairs " shall have power to take account from time to time of their children, concerning their calling and employment of their children, especially of their ability to read and understand the principles of religion * * * and to impose fines on all them who refuse to render such accounts to them when required."[2]

---

[1] Mass. Col. Rec., I., 384.
[2] Mass. Col. Records, II., 8–9.

In 1647 the Court enacted as follows:

"It being one chief point of that old deluder, Satan, to keep men from the knowledge of the Scriptures, as in former times, by keeping them in an unknown tongue so in these latter times, by persuading from the use of tongues, that so at last the true sense and meaning of the original might be clouded by false glosses of saint-seeming deceivers, that learning might not be buried in the grave of our fathers in church and commonwealth, the Lord assisting our endeavers."[3]

It was then ordered that a grammar school be set up in every town that numbered fifty or more householders. In 1652 the Court made the following recommendation:

"If it should be granted that learning, namely, skill in the tongues and liberal arts, is not absolutely necessary for the being of a commonwealth and churches, yet we conceive that the judgment of the godly wise it is beyond all question, not only laudable, but necessary for the being of the same."[4]

It was then recommended by the Court that a voluntary subscription be taken up in each town for the maintenance of the president, fellows, and poor scholars of Harvard College. In August, 1645, the inhabitants of Roxbury " in consideration of their religious care of posterity " having taken thought " how necessary the education of their children in literature will be to fit them for the public service both in church and commonwealth " unanimously agreed to erect a free school and to allow 20 pounds per annum to the schoolmaster to be raised out of the properties given by certain inhabitants of the town.[5]

These references show the close relationship between the church and the necessity of education so clearly that it is unnecessary to multiply instances—in fact there is no evidence to the contrary to be found. Nothing could be more conclusive than the enactments of the General Court which expressed the opinion of the inhabitants and in these we always get the idea that education was the natural complement of religion.

Now ten of the towns included within this study were settled previous to 1647—the year when schools were made compulsory and, as civil units, put under the control of the towns. Six of these towns, according to the records, had schools before this

---

[3] Ibid. 203.
[4] Ibid. IV., Pt. 1, 100–1.
[5] Dillway: A history of the Rox. Grammar School, 7–9.

date. The distribution of years intervening between settlement and record of a school being 4, 6, 6, 7, 9, 11—average 7. There is no mention of schools in the other four towns until after 1647; the number of years between settlement and recorded school being 16, 20, 34, 41,—average 27. Of this same group the number of years between 1647 and first record of school is 21, 14, 30, 3—average 17. Though there is no record of schools during the time indicated by the last distribution series we know that there must have been a compliance with the law or else the town would have been presented for want of a school but no evidence of such presentment—though we find many later in the century[6]—appears so far as the minutes of the town are concerned. Hence the absence of records does not mean that there were necessarily no schools. To the towns included in the first we may add the time intervening between settlement and 1647 of the four towns in the last distribution making the entire series 2, 4, 6, 6, 7, 9, 11, 11, 13, 17. Dropping the first figure, as it indicates a settlement of but two years, the average time intervening between the settlement of the town and the records of a school, or before schools were made compulsory, is 10.5 years. Does it seem probable that there were no schools during this time? Is it not clear from all the previous discussion that the Puritan religion demanded schools? We have already shown that absence of records concerning school matters does not mean absence of schools and the last word on the question is, that though actual demonstration is not possible all inference favors the hypothesis that schools existed earlier than the records indicate.

Granted that schools were in existence during this period, the question arises: Were they private schools or were they connected with the church as representing the sentiment of the town? Here again we must depend upon indirect evidence in the solution of the question. It would be unsafe to hold that there were no private schools during this period when the records are silent for the colonists were familiar with both the private and the chartered schools of England. But were the social and religious conditions favorable to the general establishment of such a type of school? The Puritan religion demanded that all chil-

[6] Dedham Records IV., 221, 214. Duxbury Records p. 206. Corey Malden Records p. 601–605.

dren be educated. We know that on account of poverty many
could not receive such education if there were only a private
school in the town and if any payment had been made by the
town to such a master for the tuition of poor children, it would
have been made a matter of record as will be seen later in the
study. Then, again, the colonists were highly homogenous and
the private school flourishes best in a mixed and individualistic
society. Logically, a school connected with the church to which
all the inhabitants belonged is the one which best fits the conditions mentioned; such a school under church organization is in
harmony with the ideas of Knox and is also in keeping with the
Welsh Education Act which we have previously quoted.

Having reasonable grounds to believe that schools did not
begin with the first recorded instance and that there was a close
relationship between these early schools and the church organization, let us now turn to the question of church support since
with this close affiliation between the church and the early school
we may expect a similarity between their methods of support.

The method which received the earliest sanction of the Church
was that of the voluntary contribution. One of the earliest references on this point bears the date of 1633: "After much delibera-
tion and serious advice, the Lord directed the teacher, Mr. Cotton, to make it clear by the Scripture, that the minister's maintenance, as well as all other charges of the church, should be defrayed out of a stock or treasury, which was to be raised out
of the weekly contribution, which was accordingly agreed upon."[7]
This method, being based more on what men ought to do rather
than on what men will do was probably found inadequate in
many cases. We find that after the synod held in 1637 Gov.
Winthrop proposed " whether, as the churches were not of one
mind on the subject of maintaining their ministers, this matter
should not now be settled" but the elders declined acting on
it.[8] In the same year the Court addressed each church as follows: " To the elders and brethren of the church at ————.
Whereas complaint hath been made to this court, that a different
course is holden in the churches for raising a treasury for maintenance of ministers, and whereupon some ministers are not so
comfortably provided as were fitting, it is desired that the several

---

[7] Felt, Ecclesiastical History of N. E., Vol. I., 173.
[8] Ibid. 319.

churches will speedily inquire hereinto, and if need be, to confer together about it, and send some to advise with this court at the next session thereof."[9]

The next year, 1638, the Court enacted as follows:

"This Court taking into consideration the necessity of an equal contribution to all common charges in towns, and observing the chief occasion of the defect herein ariseth from hence, that many of those who are not freemen, nor church members, do take advantage to withdraw their help in such voluntary contributions as are in use.

"It is therefore hereby declared, that every inhabitant in any town is liable to contribute to all charges, both in church and commonwealth whereof he doth, or may receive benefit: and withal it is also ordered, that every such inhabitant who shall not contribute proportionately to his ability with other freemen of the same town to all common charges as well for the upholding the ordinances of the churches as otherwise shall be compelled thereto by assessment and distress to be levied by the constable, or other officers of the town as in other cases."[10]

Though this gave the requisite power to the church, the idea that the church should be supported voluntarily and not through coercion was still powerful. This position, according to Winthrop, was maintained by Cotton in 1639. He holding that when congregations will not support their ministers, unless required by law, their piety is on the decline. As time went on, however, compulsion was used more and more until in 1657 but three churches in Massachusetts were being supported by voluntary contributions.[11]

The evolution of church support is clearly shown in the Records of Salem. At a general town meeting held in 1639: "There was a voluntarie towne contribution towards the maintenance of the ministry, quarterly to be paid."

"The note thereof remaineth with the deacons."[12]

By 1657 the voluntary contribution as a method of support had proved insufficient and "it was voted and agreed by the towne: that they voluntary yeald themselves to be rated: by those whom they shall choose for the Rayseing of maintenance for the ministry: When need shall require."[13] There was evidently a feeling in the town similar to that expressed by Cotton with re-

---

[9] Ibid. 331.
[10] Mass. Col. Rec., Vol. I., 240–241.
[11] Felt, Eccl. Hist. of N. E., Vol. II., 160.
[12] Salem Rec., 93.
[13] Ibid. 197.

spect to compulsion and two weeks after the above resolution was passed the town " agreed that the Elders mayntenance shalbe Indeaured to be raised by subscribcon."[14]  The result of this endeavor is shown by the following Act passed two months later: " Its ordered that all those psons that will not subscribe nor Contribute towards the Mayntenance of the ministry shalbe rated & the selectmen to rate ym."[15]  This represents a transition stage in church support.  Part of the town contributed voluntarily from a sense of religious duty; the remainder of the inhabitants contributed under compulsion or else was rated according to property valuation.

The last stage was reached in 1659 when it was " ordered that those sumes for the ministry shall be Raised vppon the town by way of Rate."[16]

In the majority of the towns studied there is no mention of church support until the method of general taxation is enforced. For example, the first record of ministerial support in Dorchester occurs in 1652; Watertown, 1648; Springfield, 1645; Dedham, 1666.  It would scarcely be held, however, that there were no churches in the towns up to the time of recorded support.  The records show that ministers were employed but the town as a civil unit was not as yet concerned with the minister's salary, hence there was no reason why town records should have been made.

From the foregoing we gather the following facts.  The first method of church support in New England was by the voluntary contribution, each according to his ability.  This soon proved unsatisfactory and in some places the ministers were in need.  The Court asked for advice and later passed an Act compelling all to contribute in proportion to ability to pay if a satisfactory amount was not voluntarily given.  This is the second method, namely, compulsory contribution.  The current having set in that direction, the transition to direct taxation of all the inhabitants, the third method, was a comparatively easy step.

The recorded actions of the towns on the matter of school support during the early period are very few and taken by themselves would not be very conclusive.  We have shown,

---

[14] Ibid. 210.
[15] Ibid. 215.
[16] Ibid. 224.

however, the logical probabilities of schools during this period and of their close connection with the church. Under these conditions the evolution of church support furnishes a basis of interpretation, a something which fills in and supplements the little evidence which we have with respect to the schools.

Boston in 1636 had a free school maintained by the voluntary contributions of forty-five of its richer inhabitants.

In the Annals of Salem, Felt states that the first schoolmaster " besides teaching assisted Mr. Peters in the pulpit, and so continued over two years." Nothing is said with respect to method of payment but as he was connected with the church and it at that time was supported by voluntary contributions the general social situation would point towards the teacher's salary being raised by the same method.

The inhabitants of Charlestown in 1636 passed the following resolution: " Mr. William Withrell was agreed with to keep a school for twelve moneth to begin the eighth of August and to have 40 pounds this year."[17] This was not a private school and was not supported by rate—public opinion was not yet ripe for such action as the general tenor of this study shows—hence it must have been supported by contribution or tuition. From the fact that tuition is not mentioned in this very direct and explicit statement and from the general social conditions during the early period it is quite probable that the subscription was used and in this case it would not be necessary to make the town action more detailed than it is.

The inhabitants of Dedham in 1644 agreed to contribute proportionately for the support of a school. This was done voluntarily but at the same time it was a compulsory measure since a fair amount would have been collected in case any of the inhabitants had refused to contribute and all must have felt the compelling force of the agreement.

Winthrop in his History of New England, 1645, states the charges of the school at Boston were met yearly by contribution either paid voluntarily or by rate on such as refused, and that other towns provided maintenance in like manner.[18]

This concludes all the available evidence on the period preceding the Act of '47 and so much of it as we have points to a

---

[17] Frothingham, History of Charlestown, 65.
[18] See Boston Records, Chap. IV.

period of voluntary contribution followed by a period of compulsory contribution. The evolution of church support which we have already traced lends the weight of corroborative evidence to the truth of the deduction. It is of course possible that in some towns the school which the town as such fostered was supported by tuition but the burden of proof is against such a statement. Tuition was no doubt charged in private schools but as a general method for the town school it logically came with the loss of communal spirit and the consequent growth of individualism. We must not think, however, of the schools that were supported by either voluntary or compulsory contributions as being free schools in our acceptance of the meaning of the term even though all children might attend free of charge. No pro rata tax was levied to support these schools on a definite evaluation of property.

# CHAPTER III

## FREE EDUCATION FOR THE POOR

In a study of poor relief and apprenticeship in Massachusetts we shall find that there was a great similarity between the laws of England and local action in the towns. In fact the law of 1642 was to all intents and purposes the apprenticeship law of Elizabeth (1601)[1] with the addition of an educational requirement. There are numerous examples in the records of apprenticeship fees being paid by the town and of a general oversight by the selectmen of those parents who apparently neglected or were unable to educate their children. As apprenticeship fees were paid by the town from a stock which was raised on all the inhabitants, so the town paid for the schooling of poor children by rate or exemption from tuition which in the last analysis was equivalent to a rate. Hence one factor in the support of a school by rate—the free school—is to be found in the Act of 1642.

In a consideration of the support of the poor in Massachusetts we must bear in mind that the evolution had already been completed in England by 1601 and that the early colonists were entirely familiar with the law and its methods. Yet the conditions peculiar to a new and undersettled country made such elaborate provisions as were customary in England quite unnecessary. In many places the poor received allotments of land for cultivation and pasturage, certain wood-lots were set off for their use, and in the early years when the communal spirit was still strong it is more than probable that neighborly hands lightened the burdens of poverty in many instances. In the nature of the case the records of voluntary contributions with the exception of gifts of land and wood must be very few. I find however that in 1641 the usual method of the Salem church was to take up a contribution each Sabbath and the deacons used the money so contributed for the support of the ministry and the poor.[2]

That great care was taken to keep the number of the poor at the minimum is seen early in the history of the colony. In

---

[1] Chap. I., p. 11.

[2] Felt, Ecclesiastical Hist. of N. E., Vol. I., 433.

the second letter of instruction to Endicott in 1629 the following admonition is given:

"Wee may not omitt, out of zeal for the general good once more to
putt you in mynde to bee very circumspect, to settle some good orders
whereby all persons resident upon our plantacions may apply themselves
to one calling or other, and noe idle drones bee permitted to live amongst
us, which, if you take care now at the first to establish, will be an undoubt-
ed meanes, through Gods assistance to prevent a world of disaster and
many grevious sins and sinners."[3]

Every town took care that no probable charge was admitted
as an inhabitant and as an example of what may be found in
any one of the town records I quote from Watertown:

"Agreed that whosoever being an Inhabitant in the Towne shall receive
any person, or family upon their property that may prove chargeable
to the Town shall maintain the said persons at their own charges."[4]

With such care exercised on the part of the towns in New
England it seems probable that during the first few years the
number of the poor was small and that the needy were helped
through church contributions and charitable individuals.

But as time went on neighborly hands were tied by their own
necessities and though the law of 1638 gave the towns the right
to compel subscriptions to all matters of public charge I can
find no instance on record of the provisions of this law being
applied to the support of the poor. It is quite possible that it
may have been in numerous instances but considering the fact
that the colonists were familiar with the methods employed in
England it would seem the natural course to adopt general
taxation either through grants from the town's stock or by
special rate as soon as the burden of support began to bear at
all heavily on the inhabitants.

In 1639 the Court assumed the " power to determine all dif-
ferences about the lawfull setling and provideing for poor persons " and " power to dispose of all unsetled persons into such
towns as they shall judge most fitt for the maintenance of such
persons and families and the most ease of the country."[5]  Doubt-
ful cases came up and the towns contested each case in a spirit
far removed from charity.  Consequently in 1645 a more definite

---

[3] Mass. Col. Rec., Vol. I., 405.
[4] Watertown Records, 1-2.
[5] Mass. Col. Rec., Vol. I., 264.

law of settlement was called for and a commission chosen " to consider the lawe for the setling of impotent aged persons, or vagrants, and either to rectifye it where it is defective, or drawe up a bill that may answer the expectation of each towne, and the whole countrye, that every towne may knowe what may be their owne burdens and prevent multiplying of peticions to this Courte hereabouts, and present their thoughts to this howse."[6]

No general order appears, however, until 1655 when complaint was made by several towns of great numbers pressing in without consent of the inhabitants and no laws to prevent it. Each town was authorized to refuse admission and every person brought into the town without consent of the selectmen should be maintained by those who were the cause of their coming in and such person or persons were obliged to give security to the town.[7]

We have already shown that support of the poor in England passed through the voluntary and the compulsory contribution stages before its final outcome in general taxation and is important to our study as throwing additional secondary evidence on the question of school support during the hazy period preceding the year 1647. Previous to a well defined theory of the power and limits of taxation these seem to have been the necessary steps. With the elimination of the second step, compulsory contribution, there is evidence on every hand in our own time of this same process. Have not the great majority of our educational and philanthropic innovations come about in the same way on the financial side? So in the case of poor support in Massachusetts all the evidence which we have indicates that relief first came through voluntary contribution on the part of the town, through the friendly disposed, and through the church contribution. There is no evidence of compulsory contribution nor is it to be expected. The right of the State to tax all the inhabitants for the support of the poor had been laid down in the mother country and the New Englander was familiar with the actual working out of the principle. When help for the needy became, therefore, a matter of moment, it was the natural thing to draw orders on the town treasury.

Let us now turn to a comparison of the method of apprenticeship. In the Massachusetts towns the first Act dealing with

[6] Ibid. Vol. III., 15.

[7] Ibid. Vol. III., 376–7.

this topic was passed by the General Court in 1642 and is as follows:

"Taking into consideration the great neglect in many parents and masters in training up their children in labor and learning and other employments which may be profitable to the Commonwealth, do hereupon order and decree that in every town the chosen men appointed for managing the prudential affairs of the same shall henceforth stand charged with the care of the redress of this evil, so they shall be liable to be punished or fined for the neglect thereof upon any presentment of the grand jurors or other information or complaint in any plantations in this jurisdiction; and for this end they, or the greater part of them, shall have power to take account from time to time of their parents and masters of their children concerning their calling and employment of their children. especially of their ability to read and understand the principles of religion and the capital laws of the country, and to impose fines upon all those who refuse to render such accounts to them when required; and they shall have power, with the consent of any court or magistrate, to put forth apprentices the children of such as shall not be able and fit to employ and bring them up, nor shall take course to dispose of them themselves; and they are to take care that such as are set to keep cattle be set to some other employment withal as spinning up on the rock, knitting, weaving tape, etc.; and that boys and girls be no allowed to converse together, so as may occasion any wanton, dishonest or immodest behavior. And for the better performance of this trust committed to them, they may divide the town amongst them, appointing to every of the said townsmen a certain number of families to have special oversight of. They are also to provide that a sufficient quantity of materials, as hemp, flax, etc., may be raised in their several towns, and tools and implements provided for workingout the same. And for their assistance in this so needful and beneficial employment, if they meet with any difficulty or opposition which they cannot well master by their own power, they may have recourse to some of the magistrates, who shall take such course for their help and encouragement as the occasion shall require, according to justice."[8]

A comparison of this Act of the Court with the general provisions of the Elizabethan law of 1601 shows the addition of and the Puritan emphasis upon reading and conduct. These in fact stand out as the emphatic points of the Massachusetts law, while the industrial feature receives the emphasis in its English fore-runner.

The Act of 1642 places the responsibility of carrying out its provisions upon the men who manage the " prudential affairs of

---

[8] Mass. Col. Records, II., 8–9.

the town " instead of the overseers of the poor, officials who came much later in Massachusetts in response to the growing number of the poor and the increased duties of the selectmen.

The provision for supplying raw material for training apprentices and to give an opportunity by which adults might turn an honest penny is identical in both laws as is also the power which is given to certain officials to apprentice such children whose parents are not able to bring them up to profitable employment.

The power to tax which is explicitly given in the English law is implicit in the Colonial measure as the selectmen are to be punished or fined in case these duties with which they are charged are not properly performed. It is not to be supposed that these officials were individually liable for the money necessary to carry out the provisions of the Act. Occasions for the exercise of these powers were probably quite infrequent and a special rate was therefore unnecessary; the required amount being taken from the levy to cover the general expenses of the town. Two. items taken from the Dorchester Records bear out the above statements.

"Artecls of Agreement had been made and agreed vpon between Captaine Hopstill Foster, Liftnt Jno Capen, Ensigne Richard Hale, Srgnt Samuell Clap and Srgnt James Blake, Selectmen of the town of Dorchester for the time being on the one part: and Henery Merefeild and Margaret his wife of the same town on the other pt'y: this three and twentieth day of March one thousand Six hundred and Sixty nine or Seaunty, as followeth:

"Wittneseth that the said Selectmen on the behalf of the Towne haue put and bound the child of John Stock and Deliuerance his wife vnto the said Henery Merefeild and Margarte his wife their heyers executors Administrators or Assignes, to Nurce, educate and bring up vntill it accomplish the age of Sixteene or eighteene yeers (at the liberty of the said Merefeild to accept of) it being now about the age of twenty weeks, finding vnto and pv'iding for the maintenance of the Child now in its Infancy.

"And soe forward as it shall grow vp to more ripeness of years and statuer duering the whole term such sufficient nessesarys for food and rayment &c. as shall be meete: as alsoe when it shall be Capable to teach or Cause it to be taught to read p'ftly the English tongue, And alsoe to teach and instruct her in the principles of Christian religion. And in such houswifry emploument of Spinning and knitting, as she may be capable off to learne and her to keep in sickness and in helth......And in Consideration heeroff the foresaid Selectmen doe in behalf of themselves for the time being and their Successors on the behalf of the Towne that ther shall be paid out of the towne Rate the Sum of Therty pounds: Viz: ten pound at the end of the feirst yeer after the date heerof whether the Child liue or dy; and ten pound by the yeer for the next two yee .; then he the said Merefeild shall haue but p'portionably of the pay ac'urd-ing to the life of the Child in witness heerof etc.''[9]

### An earlier record, 1651, is of the same import:

"It is agreed between the selectmen and br Tolman that hee shall take Henry lakes child to keepe it vntill it com to 21 yeares of age &c and therefore to haue 26 pounds and to give security to the towne and to teach it to read and wright and when it is capable if he lives the said br Tolman to teach it his trade.

"further agreed if it dies wthin 2 monthes br Tolman is to returne 21 pounds if it die at one yeares end br T. is to returne 18 pounds, etc.''[10]

### In the Watertown Records we find the following indenture bearing date of 1656:

"These are to show, that Elizabeth Braibrook widow of Watertown, hath put her daughter (with the consent of the selectmen) into the hands of Simont Tomson & his wife of Ipswich ropemaker to be as an apprentice, vntill she comes to the age of eighteen years, in wch time the sd Sarah is to serve them in all lowful Comands, & the said Simont is to teach her to reade the English Tongue, & to instruct her in the knowledge of god & his ways.''[11]

### An indenture made in Springfield, 1681, is as follows:

" ....the Selectmen of the Town of Springfield, whose names are here subscribed......Do by these prsnts set forth & put to & agree with Samuell Terry Senr his wife, his heires & assignes, to take into his family under his care tuition and Education, & for his servant Jno Matthews his Son Named Jno Matthews until the said child shal attain the age of One & Twenty years........that his the said Apprentice shal be taught wel to read the English Tongue....''[12]

### No mention is made in the indenture of an apprenticeship fee but the following record shows that the town bore the expense:

"And wheras there is about seven shillings due Samuell Terrey upon ye account of his keeping Jno Matthews his child, It was voted that the Select men pay him seven shillings out of the Townes Stocke.''[13]

### Salem in 1643 ordered that

"Joseph Harris the son of George Harris deceased shall dwell with Mr Thorndeck, both of Salem, from the first day of the sixth moneth

---

[9] Dorchester Records, 165.

[10] Ibid., 306.

[11] Watertown Records, 47.

[12] Springfield Records, Vol. II., 152.

[13] Ibid., 194.

last 43 for seuen yeares finding him meate drink & aparrell: & allowing to him fiue pounds, two pounds being already payd, and the said John Thorndeck to alow to the sd Joseph three pounds at the end of his tearme."[14]

## Malden in 1745

"Voted that Edward Wayte shall have John Ramsdell who is about five years old till he come of age and said Wayt shall have thirty pounds old tenor with him in case said Waitt wil be obliged to learne said child to read, wright and cypher and also to learne him the Shoemakers trade."[15]

Dedham in the " case ppounded respecting the reliefe of the widdow Dunckley and her children " determined to " comit the care and trust of the whole case to the select men and the Deacons who haue power to provide reliefe for them and to dispose of such childeren as they shall judge meet..........."[16]
A month later action was again taken:

"The Case respecting the Vid Dunckley and her childeren......the present trust and power is committed to (......) to dispose of her 2 eldest childeren, the boye as speedily as may be and the Girle as soone as they haue optunite if it can be put out without charge but if it require charge then to returne the case to the select men before they engage."[1]

According to the law, the selectmen were not only to apprentice poor children but they were also to take " into consideration the great neglect in many parents and masters in training up their children in learning and labor." The following quotations show that this feature of the law was not neglected:

"At a meeting of the selectmen it was agreed vnto that a warrant should be directed to the Constable to Sumon Timothy Wales and his wife, and his two lesser boys, to appeare before the select men at their next meeting, to be enquiered after Concerning their Education and improuement of their time, and Peter Lyon and his wife, and Jno Plum and Arthor Cartwright and Robert Stiles all on the same account they or some of theirs."[18]

"Arthur Cartwright (being formerly Somoned) appeared before the Select men; his answer Conserning his Sonne was, that he was about to put him apprentice to a kindsman of his that is a Sea-man and soe he was dismissed.

"The same day Robt Stiles being Somoned appeared before the Select men to answer for their idleness, and vpon examination it was found

---

[14] Records of Salem, 124.
[15] Corey, History of Malden, 402.
[16] Dedham Records, Vol. III., 197.
[17] Ibid., 203.
[18] Dorchester Records, 181.

that both hee and his wife haue not improved their time to the aduantage
of their famely as they ought and ther vpon was aduertized to reforme
or elce to be further p'ceeded with as the law requiers.

"The same day Peter Lyon appeared and gaue an accoupt that his
Sonns did follow their employment and that for the time to come he
would look dillegently after them.

"The same day Timothy Wales appeared with his sonns and could
giue noe good accoumpt of that for which he was sent for, but his words
and answers were very offensiue and Contemptuous vnto the Select
men, and therefore it was ordered, that both he and his two Sons be
againe Sumoned to appeare and to guie an accompt how he answeres
the law.[19]

"The same day John Plume appeared to answer for his negligence
in his Calling, but Could giue noe good accompt for himself, or for not
disposing of his Sonne to some Master."[20]

"At a meeting of the Select men Timothy Wales and his Sonns, being
Sumoned appeared before the Select men, and upon examination of the
boys they weer found to be very Ignorant, and not able to read, and
being admoneshed was dismissed at that time only he made some acknowl-
edgment of his offensiue words and Carridge the last day of Meeting and
that in wrighting which remains on file."

## The following appears in the Brookline Records:

"It was ordered that notice be given to the severall persens under-
written, that thay within one month after the date herof, dispose of their
severall children abroad for servants to serve by Indentures for some
term of years according to their ages and capacities, wch if they refuse
or neglect to doe, The magistrates and select men will take theire children
said children from them and place them with such masters as they shall
provide accordinge as the law provides; And that they doe accordinge
to this order dispose of their children doe make return of the names of
master and children soe put out to service, with the Indentures to the
Selectmen at the next meeting."[21]

## In Watertown:

"Willyam priest John Fisk and George Larance were warned to a
meeting of the select men at John Bigulah his house they making thier
a peerance and being found defective weer admonished for not Learning
their Children to read the english toung."[22]

"At a meeting of the select men at the house of Isaake Sterns John
Bigulah and Thomas Flag seni weer a pointed to treat with Edward
Sanderson and his wife a bought giteing a servis for the bigist of his two
least of his children wher it may be to their own content and the good

---

[19] Ibid., 181.

[20] Ibid., 182.

[21] Muddy River and Brookline Records, 67.

[22] Watertown Records, 103.

Edewcation of the child in lerning and labor and the town will be help-full to them if they desire it and to acquaint them that if themselues doe not that then the town will puive a servis for it.

"It was further agreed that the select men should goe thrugh the town in their ceueral quarters to make tryall whether children and servants be educated in Learning to read the English tongue and in the knowledg of the capitall Laws according to the Law of the Country also that they may be educated in some orthadox Catacise."[23]

In a long letter to the Court the selectmen of Lancaster state with reference to a certain Edmond Parker that:

"The townsmen from time to time hath laboured with him in Reference to his son to get him sum learning and to bring him up to some employment according as the law provides or to suffer them to doe it, but nothing would prevaile with him."[24]

In reply

"The Court commended it to the care of the Select men to inspect his family and observe their manners for the future and in case they find no amendment in those charges whereof he hath been now convicted they are then hereby ordered and impowered to dispose of the sonne to service where he may be better taught and Governed."[25]

In carrying out the provisions of this Act which made education compulsory and the selectmen, for the town, responsible for the education of the poor children it is a noteworthy fact that the first school rate levied in the town of Salem (1644) was to pay the tuition of children whose parents were unable to pay. We also quote from the Dedham Records:

"A Rate was made for the paym't of the Schoolemaster what is due from the male Childeren that are capable to paye according to the Town order being assessed at 3s-6d per childe."[26]

In 1702 Braintree

"Provided that any poor persons in this Town who shall send any children to sd school & find themselves unable to pay upon application to the Select men it shall be in their power to remit a part or ye whole of ye sum."

Brookline in 1687 enacted:

"And that the Remainder necessary to support the charge of the Master be laid equaly on the scholars heads save any persons that are poor to be abated wholly or in part."

---

[23] Ibid., 104.
[24] Lancaster Records, 95.
[25] Ibid., 96.
[26] Dedham Records, Vol. II., 125.

### In 1704 Plymouth excepted

"The Children of such as through poverty are rendered oncapable of pay theire Children to goe to school free......"

## Watertown in 1686 when changing from support by general taxation to tuition and supply

"Voated Allso that the Towne will paye for such Chilldren as thear parents are not abell to pay for the select men Being Judges of that matter."

### Boston in 1679 referred

"A Free Schoole to teach the Children of poore people to ye Select-men."

Four years later two such schools were ordered. It is probable that all the towns in which the schools were not free from tuition charges made provision for those children whose parents were unable to pay. Dedham, for example, in its formal enactments on school matters makes no such provision yet when the tuition rate is being made up we find that exceptions were made. This may be the situation in other towns whose records are silent on this point. All this action on the part of the towns indicates the far-reaching influence of the Law of 1642 which commands the town so to provide that all children shall at least be able to read. When the town made such provision by abating tuition in favor of those unable to pay, such action amounted to a poor rate since with the teacher at a fixed salary whatever amount was not met by tuition must have been paid by rate. Or, if the rate were fixed and the remainder made up by tuition, then the burden fell upon the parents who were able to pay tuition charges and became more or less a compulsory contribution. The tendency, of course, would always be to throw the burden upon the town and we may say without fear of contradiction that the first general system of free education at the expense of the taxpayers was brought about by the Act of 1642.

In summary, then, the first and last stages of development shown in the history of the support of the poor in England are indicated in the methods for a like purpose in colonial Massachusetts; also the Law enacted in 1642 and the examples of its enforcement which have been cited show how deeply its various provisions were rooted in the Poor Laws of England. The English law established the principle that the property of the State is subject to taxation that the child of poor parents may be taught to labor. The Massachusetts law broadened the scope of responsibility to include learning as well. It has been shown conclusively that the town was held responsible through the selectmen for the free education of the child and that the town met its responsibilities through apprenticing children, through warning neglectful parents, and through remitting or abating tuition charges.

# CHAPTER IV

RECORDS OF TOWN ACTION WITH RESPECT TO SCHOOL SUPPORT

In this chapter we propose to present all the data, with respect to school support up to the time when schools became supported by general taxation, which is found in the records and local histories of twenty-one Massachusetts towns.

Previous to this our conclusions have been based for the most part on the influence of an existing solution of similar problems in other fields of experience as well as on the few records bearing upon our problem, the latter being evidence that the former was an active element in the situation. But in time the direct influence of European ideals and experiences began to wane and methods of support became more adapted to local conditions. All these variations are a matter of record and from them we complete the development process and derive our conclusions to be found in a later chapter.

But somewhat in preparation for a better understanding of the records of town action and the charts of expenditures in Brookline, Dedham, Dorchester, and Watertown it seems best to discuss briefly the general method of taxation and the various activities for the support of which the townsmen were taxed.

Though it was probably used earlier, yet in 1646 the Court fixed upon 1 penny to every 20 shillings valuation as a rate sufficient to carry on the business of the Colony or "Country." This continued to be the basis of calculation though in 1655 the penny per pound lost its characteristic of being the "rate" for in that year 1¼ rates were called for and the reduplication went as high as 16 rates in 1676. The Court also in 1646 levied a poll tax of 20 pence on all males over 16 years of age, and a reduplication of the rate also called for a like reduplication of the poll tax which of course bore heavily on those with little property from which to pay. These two items constituted what was called the "Country Rate." I quote an invoice from Watertown for the year 1678 showing the basis for the distribution of taxes among the towns:

"This day the inuoice for the cuntry Reate was parfected Amounting vnto 6691 pounds & the parsons 176.

Also from the Records of Boston showing the high esteem in which the poll tax was held:

"In respect of polle money we apprehend its parallel is not in any country where the sword is not drawn in offensive or defensive war."

The various rates were usually paid in " country pay " which meant whatever kind of produce or even live stock the taxpayer had to offer. An example is taken from the Court Records for 1640:

"It was ordered, that in payment, silver plate should pass as 5s. the ounce; good ould Indian corne, growing hear, being clean and marchantable, at 5 s. the bushell, summer wheate at 7 s. the bushell, rye at 6—8 the bushell. And for horses, mares, cowes, goats, and hoggs, there is a committee appointed to valewe them under their worth rather than above their worth."

To this list we might add fish, lumber, beaver skins, wampum, and peas. A large discount was always given for cash varying from ⅓ to ½ the amount of the tax.

Rates were levied commonly for the country, the pastor, the town, the school, and infrequently for meeting such expenses of the county Court as were not paid by fines, etc. With the exception of the rate for the school these are all shown in a Watertown town order for the year 1678.

| | |
|---|---|
| A cuntry & County Reate of | 145—12—03. |
| A reate for the pasturs maintainance of | 142—18—00. |
| And a towne Rate of | 91— 8—01. |

The sources of school support mentioned in the records are the income from lands, islands, ferries, legacies, etc., contributions, tuition, and taxation. The town rates for schools were of two kinds: (1) An amount covering the master's salary, or a definitely determined part of it; and (2) an amount sufficient to meet the difference between the sum paid by the pupils and the salary guaranteed to the master. The latter rate was called " supply." We have a good example of this in the Braintree Records:

"That what ye Rent of Town Lands and ye head money of ye Schollers shall fall short of ye School masters sallery shall be raised by a Towne rate equally proportioned upon ye Inhabitants of ye sd Town."

Tuition rates were also of two kinds, (1) a fixed amount to be paid by all the children of a specified age or else by such as attended school, as for example from the Dedham Records:

"The Schoole Rate for the raiseing £25 one £5 wherof is to pay bro:
metcalf £12 10s. being by Town voate to be borne by the schollers the
other is pd by estates at 1p £ the ouer pluse whereof is to paye the Towne
debts." or again from the same town:

"A Rate made for the paymt of the Schoole Master what is due for
the male Childeren that are capable to pay according to the Town order
being assessed at 3s. 6d. p childe."

and (2) an indefinite amount to supplement a fixed town rate
as witness the agreement between the town of Newbury and the
master:

"the Selectmen agreed with Henry Short to be the schoolmaster and
to have for the first halfe yeare five pounds to be paid out of the Towne
Rate and to have sixpense a week for every scholar."

Let us now turn to our main sources of information—the records themselves.

In 1635 the Town of Boston agreed to invite " brother Phile-
mon Pormont " to become its schoolmaster[1] and in the following
year forty-five of " the richer inhabitants " contributed " toward
the maintenance of a free schoolmaster for the youth with us,
Mr. Daniel Maud being now chosen thereunto."[2] This shows
clearly that the first public school in Boston was supported by
voluntary contribution. Further evidence on this point is furnished by Winthrop in his History of New England in which
he writes that in 1645 the custom was to pay " the yearly charge
of the school by contribution, either by voluntary allowance, or
by rate of such as refused, etc., and this order was confirmed
by the General Court."[3] A probable instance of this rating of
those who refused since Winthrop mentions no general rating
is found in the records for the year '44, when it was ordered
" that the Constables shall pay unto Deacon Eliot for the use
of mr Woodbridge eight pounds due to him for keeping the
Schoole the Last yeare."[4]

With the exception of the income derived from the rental of
several islands and of a tract of land in Braintree there is no
further mention of support of the school until 1650 when at
that time it was " agreed that Mr. Woodmansey, the Schoolmaster, shall have fiftye pounds per annum for his teaching the

---

[1] Second Report of the Record Commissioners, 5.

[2] Ibid., 160.

[3] Winthrop, Hist. of N. E., II., 264.

[4] Second Report of Record Commissioners, 82.

schollers and his proportion to be made up by rate."[5]  This marks the end of the period of support by contribution, either voluntary or compulsory, and rates were levied annually from this time on.

These rates were levied, however, for the support of the Grammar School.  In 1679 agitation was begun to establish a free school for the children of the poor, that is, a school where writing and arithmetic should be taught.[6]  Four years later the following action was taken:

"At a meeting of Dr. Elisha Cooke, Mr. Simond Linde, and Mr. John Faireweather with the present Selectmen of the Town beinge a Committee apoynted by the town to consider of and provide one or more free schools for teaching of children to write and cypher accordinge to a vote of the 18th of December 1682, It was voted by the said Committee first that two schooles shall be pvided and agreed for secondlie yt the Towne shall allow 25 pounds ann for each schoole for the present & yt such psons as send thiere Children to schoole (yt are able) should pay something to ye Master for his better incouragement in his worke."[7]

This last clause shows that the schools though supported by rate were not absolutely free.  In the Selectmen's report for 1741 we see that the custom of making a charge on the individual pupil still continued.  The item referred to is as follows:

"Mr. John Proctor, Master of the North Writing School, appeared at the Desire of the Selectmen and being fully Discoursed with upon the Complaint of his refusing to take Children of some Families of Low circumstances in the World, and insisting on large Demands for Firing and Entry money etc—to which he Informed that as to Firing, he had not more than Five Shillings a piece, one with another (some paying and some not Paying) and as to the Entry money, he had not Demanded any of the Towns Inhabitants, but of Strangers, of which he now had about Ten in School, And that he has refused none of the Inhabitants children, but such as could not read the Psalter."[8]

It was ten years later, 1751, before charges of some kind on at least those pupils whose parents were able to pay were definitely forbidden.  Several of the inhabitants being dissatisfied because of the great expense to which the town was put to support the schools petitioned for the appointment of a committee to investigate the matter.  The committee reported as follows:

---

[5] Ibid., 99.
[6] The Report of the Record Commissioners, Vol. 7., 127.
[7] Ibid., 161.
[8] Records of the Selectmen of Boston, 1736-42, 288.

"The Committee appointed the 12th of March last to make Enquiry into the present state of the Town and the Couse of the great Expence thereof and to consider what Method the Town can take in order to prevent or reduce the same, now reported, that they had met and attended tht service & having Particularly Inspected the Accompts both of the Selectmen and the Overseers of the Poor, agreed upon the whole to Report as follows Vizt.

"1st. That the Charge of supporting the several publick schools amounted the last year to more than ⅓ part of the whole sum drawn by the Selectmen; but altho, this Charge is very Considerable & the number of Schools is greater than the Law requires, Yet as the Education of Children is of the greatest Importance to the Community; the Committee cannot be of the Opinion that any Saving can be made to Advantage on that head; except the Town should think it expedient to come into Methods to oblige such of the Inhabitants who send their Children to the publick Schools and are able to pay for their Education themselves to ease the Town of that Charge by assessing some reasonable Sum upon the for that purpose.

"Which being read, Voted that each paragraph of said report be taken into Consideration separatly, and by itself, and thereupon the first paragraph was Debated, and the following Question put Vizt. Whether the Town will come into any Alteration or other method than they now have relating to the Schools ...... Voted in the Negative.

"On a motion made and seconded, Voted that the several Masters of the Publick Grammar Schools and Writing Schools in the Town be directed not to refuse taking into their respective schools any Child, or Children, that may be brought to 'em, for Education, in Case Enterence Money (so called) is not paid said Masters, and allso that they shall not demand any Pay or Allowance for Instructing such Children, as belong to the Town, and that attend in the School hours only."[9]

This to all intents and purposes made the schools of Boston entirely free.

The first method of support for the town school of Braintree is shown by an act passed in 1668 which is as follows:

"At Towne meeting this vote passed for schoolmaster: That the Towne of Brantry did consent to lay the Schoole land: that is to say the annuall Income of it; for a salliry for a School master, and to make it up to twenty pounds besides what every child must give."[10]

In '79 the salary of the master was made thirty pounds but the method of support indicated above was not changed.[11]

In '81 both the rent and the rate were made definite sums:

---

[9] The Report of the Record Commissioners, Vol. 14., 199.
[10] Records of the Town of Braintree, 9.
[11] Ibid., 18.

" the rent as formerly at 15 lb. & fifteen pounds by a Towne rate."[12]   No mention is made here of tuition charges but as his salary in '79 was thirty pounds beside the " quarter money " it is probable that the action taken in '81 did not make the school free but merely defined what was expected from the town and from the school lands.   In 1700 the tuition charge was one shilling per quarter[13] which evidently was paid with considerable reluctance as is shown by the direction given by the town to the selectmen in 1701.

''It was then voted that the Selectmen shalbe and are now empowered to call for and recover ye Entry money......for ye yeare 1700 & 1701 by suit at law upon refusal of yr Parents or masters concerned.''[14]

The above action would indicate a considerable difference of opinion in the town with respect to the proper method of support and it was probably on this account that the town later in the year set forth at length the views of the majority in the following resolution:

''The Inhabitants of Braintry Regulerly Asembled for the setling of a Schoolmaster or Schoolmasters for ye year ensuing and raising of their sallary or Sallerys and a suitable way for ye paying of it—First voted that ye Rent of ye Towne lands formerly paying to ye school shall continue a part of ye Sallery. 2. That ye parent or master that shall send any scholler or schollers to ye said school shall pay for each Scholler or schollers to ye Town Treasr for ye support of ye school five shillings a yeare & Proportionably for any part of it.

''3. That any Person or Persons living out of ye Towne who shall send any Scholler or Schollers to ye aforesd School shall pay twenty shillings a year to ye Town Treasr and proportionably for any part of it. Provided that any poor persons in this Town who shall send any children to sd school & find themselves unable to pay upon application to the Select men it shall be in their power to remit a part or ye whole of ye sum.

''4. That what ye Rent of Town Lands and ye head money of ye Schollers shall fall short of ye School masters sallery shall be raised by a Town rate equally proportioned upon ye Inhabitants of ye sd Town.

''Then voted yt Lt John Baxter & Lt Samuel Penniman should carry what has been voted and agreed upon to ye next sessions and offer it to them for their approbation and confirmation.''[15]

No record was made of the Court's decision nor is there any record of the town's action with respect to schools until 1716.

---

[12] Ibid., 20.

[13] Ibid., 47.

[14] Ibid., 50.

[15] Ibid., 51.

It was then voted " by ye Inhabitants of Braintry Regularly assembled that there should be a school kept in the South end of this Town for one half of the year, each year yearly, beginning the first day of October yearly, for reading & writing (besides the present grammar school) and that to be at the charge of the town."[16]   Whether this action marks the beginning of school support by general taxation or whether it began at some earlier date can not be decided from the records but as will be shown in another chapter the inference is that the year 1716 marks the date of such support.

Brookline was originally a part of the town of Boston and as such contributed to the general town expenses.  Feeling that they were not sharing in the benefits to an amount equal to their contributions, the inhabitants of the hamlet petitioned the town to be set apart.  Nine months later, December, 1686, the town took the following action:

"In answer to the petition of the Inhabitants of Mudie River, praying to have liberty to erect a school &c. upon the hearinge therof, The President and Councill doe order, That henceforth the said Hamlet of Mudie River be free from Town Rates to ye Towne of Bostone, they maintaining thoire own high wayes and poor and other publique charges ariseing among themselves, And that within one year next comeing they raise a school house in such place as the two next Justices of the Countrie shall determine as also maintaine an able reading and writinge Master there, frm and after that day, and that the Inhabitants annuallie meete and choose three men to manage thiere affairs."[17]

The following year the inhabitants

"Voted that for the Annual maintainance of the Schoolmaster twelve pounds per annum in or as money be Raised equally by a Rate according to the usual manner of Raising publick charges by the three men And that the Remainder necessary to support the charge of the Master be laid equally on the scholars heads save any persons that are poor to be abated wholly or in part."[18]

Some time previous to 1700 the hamlet evidently lost its independent position as is shown by this action of the town:

"Upon the petition of the Inhabitants of muddiriver To be a District or Hamlet seperate from the Town for these reasons following, namely, the remoteness of their situation wch renders them uncapable of Injoy-

---

[16] Ibid., 88.
[17] Muddy River and Brookline Records, 57.
[18] Ibid., 86.

ing Equal Benefit & advantage wth other of the Inhabitants of Publick Schools.

"Their petition being read & the reasons given therin Debated, It was voted in the negative, & that they had not for some time been rated in the Town rate yet for the time to come the selectmen should rate them in the Town Tax as the other Inhabitants & as formerly they used to be.

"And for their Incouragement It was voted that the Selectmen should provide a Schoolmaster for them, To teach their children to read, write & cypher & order his pay out of the Town Treasury."[19]

By 1705, Brookline was again taking local action with respect to its own affairs and the method of school support outlined in '87 was reinacted.[20] In 1710 pressure was brought to bear on the town by the outlying inhabitants and it was

"Voted That there be Liberty Granted to Erect Two Schoolhouses at there own Charge that improve them. Also that they maintain a good school dame half of the yeare at each house. That the Town allow the charge for a Master one qr at one school house and the other quarter at the other. To teach to write and Cypher."[21]

From 1710 to 1713 school was kept in two places and from that date to 1727 in three places and thereafter to the end of the printed records in two places. After the installation of the moving school there is no mention of tuition.

In the charts which follow abscissas give the years and the ordinates the amounts in pounds.

A considerable rise in the church rate indicates that a church or a house for the pastor had been built. The former is the case in Dorchester in '79, Dedham in '74 and Watertown in '54-'58 by installments; the latter in Dorchester in '82.

A rise in the province rate in the neighborhood of '75 shows the increased taxation due to King Philip's War and in '90 to King William's War.

The first schools of Cambridge were not town but private schools, the town granting the use of land or small sums of money from time to time for the "encouragement" of the master. Thus in 1638 the use of two and two-thirds acres of land was granted to Nathaniel Eaton as long as he kept school in the town.[22] In '48 the town sold some of the common land for

---

[19] Ibid., 63.
[20] Ibid., 90.
[21] Ibid., 96.
[22] The Records of the Town of Cambridge, 33.

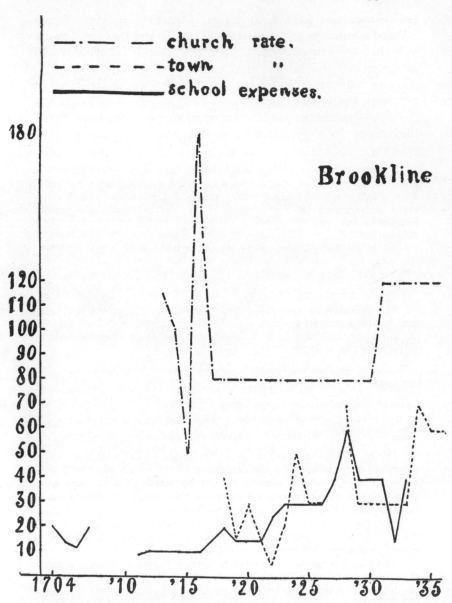

—·—— church rate.

———— town "

———— school expenses.

180

Brookline

120
110
100
90
80
70
60
50
40
30
20
10

1704    '10    '15    '20    '25    '30    '35

In the Brookline chart the abscissas give the years and the ordinates amounts in pounds. The increased church rate indicated by the rapid rise of the line in 1714–16 was due to the building of a new " meeting-house." In 1723 it was voted that three school houses be built and the necessary funds taken from the town treasury, from time to time, by order from the selectmen. In 1727 the teaching staff was enlarged by the addition of another master for a term of four months, and a school dame for a term of eight months.

ten pounds and gave it to Master Corlet.[23]  In 1654 it was
" Voted affirmative at the meeting of the Towne that the Townsmen shall levy twenty pounds upon the severall Inhabitants and
give mr Corlet for his pnt Incouragement to continue with us."[24]
All this indicates a lively interest on the part of the town in
a private not a town school.

It is not until 1692 that the recorded action of the town shows
the change from private to town school.  The record is as
follows:

"It was then voted by the Inhabitants that they would giue to a
grammar schoolmaster that should alsoe teach english that they would
allow a Schoolmaster Twenty pound ayeare in Comon pay and this was
voted in the afirmitive by the major part of the Inhabitants then present
at least two to one."[25]

The town continued to support the school in this way.

The first item of interest in the records of Dedham concerning school affairs is found in the proceedings for the year 1642:

"Also it was with vnanimous consent concluded that some portion of
land in this entended deusion should be set apart for publique vse: viz
for the Towne the Church & A fre Schoole viz: 40 acres at the least or
60 acres at the most."[26]

Most of the towns made identical provision at some time or
another and, as in the case of Dedham, disposed of the land
before it ever became a source of revenue.

No further action was taken with respect to a school until
1644 when the inhabitants passed the following resolution:

"The sd Inhabitants takeing into Consideration the great necessitie of
prouiding some meanes for the Education of the youth in or sd Towne
did with an vnanimous consent declare by voate their willingness to
promote that worke promising to put too their hands to prouide maintainance for a Free Schoole in our said Towne.

"And farther did resolute & consent testefyinge it by vote to rayse
the some of Twenty pounds p annu: towards the maintaining of a schoole
mr to keep a free Schoole in our said Towne.

"And also did resolue & consent to betrust the sd 20 pounds p annu:
& certaine lands in or Towne formerly set a part for publique use: into
the hands of Feeofees to be presently Chosen by themselues to imploy

---

[23] Ibid., 77.

[24] Ibid., 106.

[25] Ibid., 297.

[26] Dedham Records, Vol. III., 92.

the sd 20 pounds and the land aforesaid to be improved for the vse of the sd Schoole: that as the profits shall arise from the sd lands euery man may be proportionably abated of his some of the sd 20 pounds aforesaid freely to be giuen to ye vs aforesaid And yt said Feeofees shall haue power to make a rate for the necessary charg of improuing the sd land: they giueing account thereof to the Town or to whom they should depute.''[27]

We have here a free school which the youth of the town might attend; a school supported by the entire tax-paying body though not supported by a tax; a school supported by a " voluntary contribution " on the part of each inhabitant but so enacted as to make the payment as compulsory as an assessed tax; the first free school in America to be supported by the people as a whole.

In 1648 it was resolved by general consent to build a school house.[28] This was paid for out of the town rate and from the items in the constable's report apparently cost eleven pounds.

No further action was taken on the part of the town until 1651 when, the seven year covenant made in '44 having expired, it became necessary to take up the matter of support once more. At a general meeting of the town it was

" Resolved that a Schoole for ye education of ye youth in our Towne shall be continued and mayntane for the whole term of seven years next. and that the settled mayntenance or wages of the Schoole mr shall be 20 pounds p ann at ye leaste.

"A Towne stock shall be raysed to ye sume of 20 pounds at ye leaste.''[29]

The above record bears no date other than the year. What is evidently a later record of the same year reads as follows:

"It is Resolued that a Schoole for the education of youth shall be continued and mayntayned in our Towne its resolued that som settled way of the maintenance of the Schoole shall be agreed vpon.

"Its ordered that 20 pounds a yeare at the leaste shall be the settled recompence of the schoolemr for 7 yeares next ensueing

"the 5 men heerevnder named ar chosen to ripen this case of reyseing 20 pounds pan for the schoolemr and ppose thier thoughts to ye Towne.''[30]

Soon after this resolution was passed, a meeting of the selectmen was called and the following method of raising the master's

---

[27] Ibid., 105.
[28] Ibid., 123.
[29] Ibid., 135.
[30] Ibid., 192.

salary was decided upon—a method radically different from that
which founded the school seven years previously:

"Concerning the Schoole. these ppositions ar to be tendered to the
consideration of the Towne for the mayntayning therof for 7 yeares.

"1 that all such Inhabitants in our Towne that haue Male children or
seruants in thier families betwixt the age of 4 and 14 yeares shall paye
for each such to the Schoolemr for the time beinge or to his vse at his
assignment in Towne in Currant payement the sume of 5 shillings yearely
pvided that such children be then liueing and abideing in our Towne.

"2 And wt so euer these sumes fall short of the sume of Twentie pounds
shall be raised by waye of Rateing vpon estates according to the vsall
manner.

"3 that these sumes shall be payed in 2 equall sumes at the end of
each half yeare for the space of 7 yeares next ensueing."[31]

There is no record to the effect that the Town accepted these
propositions which the selectmen tendered but the fact that this
method with varying tuition rates prevailed for more than thirty
years is sufficient evidence of its acceptance.

During these years the town had been growing; homes had
been set up farther and farther away from the schoolhouse and
these estates were taxed at the same rate and the children paid
the same tuition as did those who lived near the school. This
probably seemed unfair to those less fortunately situated with
respect to the school; at any rate a different method of support,
or rather a variation of the preceding method, went into effect
in 1685 which exempted all those who lived more than two
and one-half miles from the school from paying any tuition
but taxed all such estates towards payment of one-half the school
charges. It is a most original method of dealing with the problem
and with one exception is self-explanatory. The method is as
follows:

"1 that the one half of the Schoole charges as well for quality as quantity
Shall be raised upon the ratable Estate of our inhabitants whether nearer
the school or further of.

"2 that all such persons as dwell within one mile and A quarter from
the School haveing male children Shall pay for each Such child five
Shillings A year from six years old to twelve years old.

"3 that those that dwell within two miles and A half of the Schoole,
and beyond the mile and quarter Shall pay two Shillings Six pence A
year for their male children from Seaven years old to twelve years old.

"4 that gramer Scholors Shall be rated and pay to the Schoole five

---

[31] Ibid., 202.

Shillings pr head mor then English Scholers that dwell within A mile and a quarter of the Schoole.

"5 that those inhabitants that dwell mor than two miles and A half from the Schoole Shall be freed from all charges by rates upon their childrens heads for the Schools until they Shall receive benifir thereby, and then Shall be rated and pay as those within A mile and quarter: all wayes prouided that such childrin be taken care of, so that they shall be Sufitiantly taught to read and wright.

"6 that the one halfe of tne Schoole charge Shall be raised upon the heads of the children according to those rules of proportion mentioned above."[32]

The principle of equalization for studies and for distance at the basis of this method is simple and just enough but one of the concrete instances is rather puzzling. Why were those children who lived at the greatest distance obliged when they attended school to pay the same tuition as did those who lived nearest? The only explanation that offers itself, is that on account of the distance and the danger only the older children were able to attend school and that they were " gramer Scholors." So far as the younger children were concerned it was an excellent method to keep them at home.

Besides this attempt at equalization two further points should be noted. It is implied in the fifth section that all children except those living beyond the two and a half mile limit are rated whether attending school or not; and that all children shall either at home or at school be taught to read and write. This method of rating all estates for one-half the school charges and combining with this a compulsory tuition charge whether children were in attendance or not was a long step toward complete support by taxation alone. Taxation of those who lived at such a distance that their younger children could have no advantage of the school was no doubt influential in bringing about the moving school and later the school district.

In 1691, it was decided that a return be made to the method of '51, that is, a fixed charge on each boy between 4 and 14 and the remainder to be raised on estates.[33] This continued until 1694 when the following resolution was passed:

"It being then proposed to the town whither the one half part of the Salary for the maintinance of the Schoole Shall be upon the parents or

---

[32] Ibid., Vol. V., 164.
[33] Ibid., Vol. V., 192.

masters of Such male childrn as live within three miles of the meeting house or there abouts of the agg of seuen years & under twelve years old for this present assessment. This was voted in the afermative.

"It being further proposed to the Town whither the other half part of the above mentioned sum shall be levied upon estates only and no part of it upon heads this was also voted in the afirmative."[34]

Later in the same year it was: " Also proposed to the Town whither thay will raise maintinance for the Schoole only upon persons and estates of the inhabitants. this was voted in the affirmative."[35]  As there are no records showing a change from this method of support by general taxation we may conclude that from 1694 on, the children of the town of Dedham were free from tuition charges as they were during the first seven years of the school's history.

School history in the town of Dorchester begins with this record:

"It is ordered the 20th of May 1639, that there shall be a rent of 20 pounds yeerely foreuer imposed vpon Tomsons Iland to bee payd p'euy p'son that hath p'prtie in the said Iland according to the p'portion that any such p'son shall fro tyme to tyme injoy and posess there, and this towards the mayntenace of a schoole in Dorchestr this rent of 20 pounds yeerly to bee payd to such a schoolemaster as shall undertake to teach english Latin and other tongues, and also writing the sayd schoolemaster to be chosen fro tyme to tyme p'the freemen and that is left to the discretion of the elders and the 7 men for the tyme being whether maydes shalbe taught with the boys or not. For the levying this 20 pounds yeerely fro the p'ticuler p'sons that ought to pay that according to this order. It is further agreed that some man shallbe appointed p'the 7 men for the tyme being to Recuie that and on refusall to levye that p'distresse, and not finding distresse, such person as so refuseth payment shall forfeit the land he has in p'prietie in the sayd Iland."[36]

Nothing is said in this resolution concerning tuition and it is evident from what we know about the salaries of the early schoolmasters that this rent of 20 pounds would have met all the financial needs of the school. There was trouble, however, in the collection of the rent as is shown by the following:

"Whereas the Inhabitants of Dorchester haue formerly consented and agreed that a Rate of Twentie pound p' annum shall issue and be payd by the sayd Inhabitants and their heires from and out of a certain porcon of land in Dorchester Called Tomsons Iland for and towards the main-

[34] Ibid., 226.

[35] Ibid., 209

[36] Fourth Report of the Boston Record Commissioners, 39.

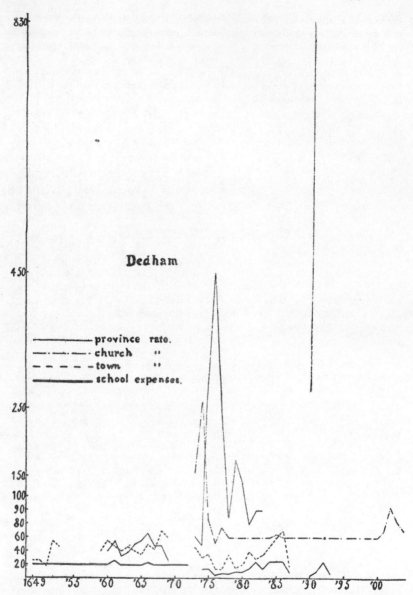

Dedham

Reference to payment of the minister comes comparatively late in Dedham. The beginning of the curve showing church expenses marks the building of a church. The first increase in the province rate was due to King Philip's War and the second, in 1790, to King William's War. The effect of the former on town and school expenses is clearly shown by the fall in the respective curves; it seems to have had no effect on church expenses. It will be observed in these charts that the various curves keep the same relative position; the main item of expense being the support of the ministry, then the province rate, then town expenses, and, lastly, the support of the school.

enance of a schoole in Dorchester aforsayd. And that upon experience it is found to be a matter of great labor and difficulty to collect the said rent from soe many severall p'sons that haue title to land in sayd Iland and who therefore ought to pay the sayd rent beinge noe lesse in number than six score or thereaboute......It is heerby ordered and all the present Inhabitants of Dorchester aforesayd Whose names are heervnto subscribed doe for themseules a and there heires heerby Covenant consent and agree that from hence forth the sayd Iland and all the benefill and prfitts thereof and all there right and Interest in he same shalbe wholy¦and foreuer bequeathed nd given away from themselues and their heires vnto the Town of Dorchester aforesayd for and towards the maintenance of a free schoole in Dorchester aforsayd for the Instructinge and Teaching of Children and youth in good literature and Learningc.''[37]

A committee was appointed and the Island put out for rent but whatever the revenue may have been the town did not long enjoy it, as the General Court revoked its grant to Dorchester and gave title to John Tomson upon his presenting proof that his father settled the Island in 1626.

In 1645, an elaborate code of rules and provisions covering all school matters was put in practice. By the first provision three men were chosen for life to act as wardens of the school.

"Secondlie, the said Wardens shall haue full power to dispose of the Schoole stock whether the same bee in land or otherwyse, bothe such as is already in beeing and such as may by any means hereafter added: and shall collect and Receiue the Rents, Issues and p'fitts arising and growing frpm sayd stock, And the sayd rents Issues and p'fitts shall lay out and imply only for the best behoof and aduantage of the sayd schoole; and the furtherance of learning thereby, and shall give a faythful¦ and true accoumpt of there receipts and disbursements so often as they shalbe therunto required by the Inhabitants or the maior p'te of them.

"Fowerthly so often as the sayd Schoole shallbe supplied with a Schoolemr—so p'vided and admitted, as aforesayd the wardens shall fro tyme to tyme pay or cause to be payd vnto the said Schoolmr such wages out of the Rents, Issues and p'fitts of the Schoole stock as shall of right come due to be payd.

"Fiuethly the sayd Wardens shall from tyme to tyme see that the Schoole howse be kept in good and sufficient repayre, the Chargs of whaich reparcion shalbe defrayed and payd out of such rents, Issues and p'fitts of the Schoole stocke, if there be sufficient or else of such rents as shall arise and grow in the time of the vacancy of the Schoolemr —if there be any such and in defect of such vacancy the wardens shall repayre to the 7 men of the Towne for the tyme beeing who shall haue power to tax the Towne for such some or sommes as shallbe requisite for the repayring of the School howse as aforesayd.

[37] Ibid., 104–5.

"Sixthly the sayd Wardens shall take care that euy yeere at or before the end of the 9th moneth their bee brought to the School howse 12 sufficient Cart, or wayne loads of wood for fewell to be for the vse of the Schoole master and the Schollers in winter the Cost and Charge of which sayd wood to bee borne by the Schoolers for the tyme being who shalbe taxed for the purpose at the discretion of the Wardens.

'Lastlv the sayd Wardens shall take care that the Schoolemr for the tyme oemg doe faythfully p'forme his dutye in his place as schoolmrs ought to doe as well in other things as in those whic are hereafter expressed, viz.

"5ly hee shall equally and impartially receiue, and instruct such as shalbe sent and Comitted to him for that end whither their parents bee poore or rich not refusinge any who haue Right and Interest in the Schoole."[38]

In a code of school procedure which goes into the minutest details it seems improbable that so important an item as tuition rates or the giving of power to the wardens to make a general levy on the inhabitants for school support would have been omitted had either method been in mind. As we know from the records that the income from Tompson's Island was insufficient, the balance of the master's salary was in all probability made up by contributions from public spirited citizens or by the inhabitants as a whole.

It is not until 1651 that we find further record of the school and this may in part at least be explained by the following:

"For as much as at the last Genall meeting the day and year abouesaid (28–9–'53)their was offence taken that the Record of the disbursements of the towne rates for the yeare 52 and 53 was not so punctuall as was desired and conseived to be the neglect of the Select men then a being which som of us confesse might haue been more playne had it been minded; a greater falt would it haue ben if their had ben no record at all, as in the yeares 45: 47 : 48 : the is none in the book to be found."[39]

It is quite possible that the omissions may have extended to the acts of the town or to the wardens of the school for the following acts of the town bear the date 1651 and indicate previou3 action of which there is no record.

"The 4th of June 1651 It was noted at a town meeting that the select men together with Mr Jones and Deacon Wiswall should forthwith treate and agree with Mr henry Butler for to teach schoole in dorchester which was accordingly agreed on as it is at the end of the booke showed the

[38] Ibid., 64–5.
[39] Ibid., 317.

agreement."[40]   In February of the same year "Mr. Butler desired that the scole rate may be gathered with the towne  rate."[41]

A school rate of 30 pounds was levied during the early part of the year, which was separate from the other town rates and as this method does not occur again for some time it is probable that the request was granted.[42]   Probably it was more difficult to collect a school rate, as such, than to add the amount of the master's salary to the town budget.

Mr. Butler was engaged to teach the school for four months of the following year at the rate of 30 pounds per annum and was paid from the town rate.[43]

All mention of school matters are dropped completely from the records for three years.  During the last month of the year '55 an agreement was made between the selectmen and Ichabod Wiswall to teach the school for a term of three years for twenty-five pounds per year, the selectmen agreeing to pay or cause the said sum to be paid to the master.[44]  The records show that the master was paid for his first year's work from the town rate 23-3-11; for the second year 22-18-6; and for the third year a rate for town and school of 30 pounds was levied but there is no record of disbursement.  As these amounts were paid from a rate levied expressly for town and school there can be no question that the amounts stated were paid by general taxation.  With a salary of 25 pounds and the town rate payment so closely approximating that amount, it seems improbable that there was a tuition charge to make up so small a deficiency. It is suggested as a very probable explanation of the manner in which the deficiency was met that the master was a resident of the town and as his father was a considerable landholder and from the records manifestly concerned in the collection of his son's salary, without doubt his taxes were turned " on account " and the balance paid along from time to time as is indicated by a record of disbursement in the year '61, three years after the contract had expired: " It to Thomas Wiswall as remainder

---

[40] Ibid., 304.
[41] Ibid., 306.
[42] Ibid., 307.
[43] Ibid., 313, 314, 316.
[44] Ibid., 73–4.

of his sonnes schoolinge 0-18-6.[45] This indicates that the town has settled the 25 pound salary in full.

It is necessary, however, to take into consideration an item of record in the year '58 which directs one of the selectmen " to look vpe what notes and papers he hath that concernes the accounts of the scollers for the two yeares past 56: and 57: and bring them to the selectmen."[46] From the preceding facts it seems improbable that these accounts could have related to tuition charges. The sixth section of the school code of '45 offers a possible explanation in that the pupils were expected to pay for the wood and it is not unreasonable to conceive that this section was still in force. At any rate, we can consistently hold that these accounts, whatever they may have been for, were not tuition charges.

Without indicating any change in the method of support the town in '59 voted to keep a school as in former times and Mr. Pole, the new master, was paid 25 pounds from the town rate.[47] With the exception of the year '69, when the master was hired for but two months, school was kept continuously from '59 to '72 at a standard wage of 25 pounds and this sum was always paid from the town rate. There is no record of school or disbursement for the year '72. In the following year the proposition was made and accepted that a schoolmaster be procured and as a rate for 50 pounds was made for town and school in the early part of '74 it is probable that a master was secured for the previous year. In '75 the constable's accounts show an item of 20-16-0 as having been paid to the master but as there is no report of the second constable's disbursements of his half of the rate collected the deficiency is readily accounted for. In '76 the master's salary was increased to 30 pounds. In '78 there is no mention of teacher or wages but a lock was secured for the schoolhouse door. Without following details longer we may say that, with the exception of three years school was maintained to the year '85, when the printed data with respect to the school ends; and the master was paid from the town rate.

I have gone into the details of school support in Dorchester because it is the one exception to the general rule of develop-

---

[45] Ibid., 107.

[46] Ibid., 94.

[47] Ibid., 97, 107, 111, 115, etc.

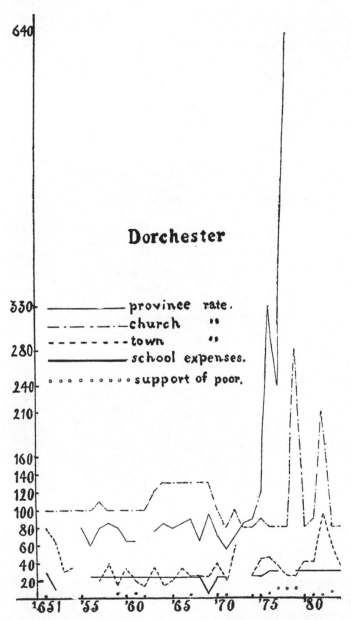

Dorchester

province rate.
church    "
town    "
school expenses.
support of poor.

The first rise in the curve of church support is due to the increased expenditure necessitated by hiring an assistant to the pastor; the second rise, in '79, to the building of a church; and the last, in '82, to building a house for the pastor. The rise in province rate was caused by King Philip's War. From the point

ment. Several other towns; apparently under the influence of that clause of the law which allowed taxation of all the inhabitants for the support of those activities which were for the benefit of all, also supported schools soon after the passage of the law of '47 by general taxation but such towns soon changed to the method of tuition and town rate. Apparently Dorchester did not make this change.

Dudley, organized in 1732, established a school seven years later by the following act:

"Voted by the said Inhabetance to raise twenty pounds of money to defray the charges of schooling. the senter of the Town To have thiere share of the abovsd money and allso each end of the Town to draw thiere proportion of the money and to lay it out in schooling thiere children."[48]

The first mention of school matters in the records of Duxbury states that the town has been fined five pounds by the Court of Quarter Sessions for want of a schoolmaster and that the town wishes to hire the money to meet the fine.[49] In the same year, 1709, a schoolhouse was built in the lower end of the town which would indicate a moving school but nothing is said concerning the method of support until 1734. The record is as follows:

"They also voted that there should be paid of the said town's money fifteen pounds one shilling and six pence more than the thirty pounds already ordered in full satisfaction to Jonathan Peterson Jr. for his services in the said town, as schoolmaster."[50]

One may reasonably infer that the school was supported by rate at this time but for how long a period this had been the customary method can not be decided from the records.

In 1741 occurs the next recorded action that the school is free:

"At this town meeting the town voted that the said town should continue to stand divided in four parts or quarters according to a former vote of the said town, as of said town records may appear, relating to the keeping of their school for the term of twenty years next ensuing. They also voted that the inhabitants of each of the said quarters respectively should provide houseroom for the said schoolmaster, while he keeps school in their respective quarters, also that the said school shall be a

---

[48] Town Records of Dudley, 76.
[49] Records of the Town of Duxbury, 206.
[50] Ibid., 244.

free school for the whole town for any of the said inhabitants to send their children into any of the above mentioned quarters where the school may be kept."[51]

There is no record of any change in method up to 1770 when the printed records stop.

Fitchburg, originally a part of Lunenburg, was organized as a town in 1764. In the same year the town voted

"That there be two Scools in sd Town & that mr John Fitch & Kindal Boutwell & their neighbors shall have the benefitt of their scoole money in order to provide scooling among themselves.

"Voted that Eight pounds be Raised in order to provide a scool master in sd Town."[52]

A schoolmaster was employed in Haverhill in 1661 at a salary of 10 pounds per annum to be paid by the town. It is quite probable that tuition was charged. The next record with respect to the school is of an act in 1670 by which the town agrees to give the master ten pounds annually to be rated on the inhabitants and in addition the master is to have what he and the parents may agree upon. In 1673 the annual amount paid by the town was "taken off, & no more to be allowed or rated for."

Nothing further appears on the records until 1685 though the Court records show that the town was presented for want of a master in 1681. It is probable that there was no regular school during this time. In '85 the selectmen were empowered to hire a master provided that they did not agree "to give him on the public account more than Four pounds in corn."

In 1711 the selectmen were ordered to hire a master who was "to move quarterly to such places as the Selectmen agree to, as shall be most convenient for the inhabitants of the town." But when through inability of the selectmen to secure a teacher willing to keep a moving school, a proposition was submitted to the town to pay a master five pounds to keep school for a quarter at the town schoolhouse it was voted down. As a petition was received the following year from inhabitants living at some distance asking for a schoolhouse and schooling at the town's cost for one quarter per year "that they might have the benefit of having their children brought up to learning as well

[51] Ibid., 270.
[52] History of the Town of Fitchburg, 7.

as the children of those who live in the center of the town," the defeat of the proposition of the previous year may well be attributed to those who would not have received benefit from the money paid to support the central school. The petition was granted and from the sources of information at hand there is no further mention of tuition charges.[53]

"At a legal meeting of the freeholders and other Inhabitants of ye Town of Lunenburg assembled December 11th, 1732:

"It was voted that Coll. John Willard Capt Edward Hartwell and Mr Benjamin Goodridge be a Commtte to Provide a School and School-master for to teach Children and youth to Read and write & if the Commtte See Good to hire a Gramer School master they shall have the liberty Provided they pay yr over Plus Charge of what ye keeping of a Gramer School would be more yn ye charge of Keeping an English School."[54]

It would seem probable that the school was supported by the town so far as the teaching of English was concerned but that the community would not tax itself that a few might learn Latin at an additional expense. Whether those interested paid the "over Plus Charge" or not cannot be determined from the records.

In 1733 a committee was appointed to provide a "Lawfull School" at three different places in the town[55] and two months later the town "Voted and Granted ye sum of Fourty Pounds for ye Charge of a School for ye year past and Present."[56]

The recorded history of schools in the Town of Malden begins with the statement that the town had been presented to the Court for want of a school—this was in 1671.[57] No further reference to schools is made until '91 when a record states that Ezekiel Jenkins continues to be the "Townes Scoule Master."[58] In '99 John Sprague was chosen schoolmaster and it was left with the selectmen to give him something for his "incouragment."[59] In 1701 the town was again presented for want of a school.

[53] History of Haverhill, Chase, pp. 113, 116, 135, 142, 236–238.
[54] Lunenburg Records, 77.
[55] Ibid., 85.
[56] Ibid., 86.
[57] The History of Malden, 601.
[58] Ibid., 602.
[59] Ibid., 602.

During this period of more than twenty-five years no mention is made of the manner of support. It is quite probable that the school kept by Jenkins, Sprague, and others was a private and not a town school but that the town gave this master of a private school a small sum for his encouragement and thus avoided a fine by the Court.

Following this second presentment the town was stirred to action and chose John Sprague " scool-master for ye yeer jnsuing To learn Children & youth to Reed and wright and to Refmetick according to his best skill. And he js to have ten pounds paid him by ye town for his pains. The scool js to be free for all ye Inhabitants of ye Town: and to be kept at foure severall places at foure severall times one quarter of a yeer jn a place: In such places whar those five men shall appoint, namly.......  who are chosen by the Town for that purpose."[60]

The following year, '02, the town changed the plan completely. Instead of a moving school it was voted to have a fixed school to be held at the master's home and instead of a free school supported by general taxation it was decided to pay the master by rate and tuition.[61] This method prevailed until 1710 when the selectmen agreed with Moses Hill " to sarue for the benifit of ye scollars," that is, for tuition receipts alone.[62] In less than a month the town was presented for not having a grammar school. But as the Selectmen proved to the satisfaction of the Court that there were but ninety-seven tax-payers the charge was dismissed and the Court ordered that the town provide itself with a school-master able to teach the children to read and write.[63]

A week later the town hired a master and voted for a moving school but for some reason a difference arose about terms. During the next month the town made two more attempts to engage a master and failed. In November, two months later, Samuel Wigglesworth was hired. Before he began his term it was voted that the " Schoole shall be kept ye first four months jn mr parsons house And then ye Schoole shall be Remoued jnto some house Towards ye North end of The Town ye othar

[60] Ibid., 602.
[61] Ibid., 603.
[62] Ibid., 603.
[63] Ibid., 606.

Two months."[64]   A town rate was made the following February and there is no record of further tuition charges.

The first schoolmaster in Newbury was employed in 1639 and received for encouragement in his work four acres of upland and six acres of salt marsh.   The records throw no further light on the method of support until 1652 when it was voted by the major part of the town " that here should be a convenient house built for the school.   There was also voted that there should be twenty pounds a yeare allowed for to maintain a schoolmaster out of the Towne rate."

In the following year

"There was ordered & voted that the towne should by an equall proportion according to mens estates by way of rates pay foure and twenty pounds by the yeare to maintain a free schoole to be kept at the meeting house & the master to teach all such inhabitants children as shall be sent to him so soon as they know their letters & begin to read."

No further record occurs until 1675.   During this time the method of support is uncertain as the town records for a number of the intervening years have been destroyed.   The record referred to is as follows:

"That whereas the Law requires that our Towne should maintaine a Grammer schoole & a schoole master to teach to recite & read, the Selectmen agreed with Henry Short to be the schoolmaster and to have for this first halfe yeare five pounds to be paid out of the Towne Rate and to have sixpence a week for every scholar."

By 1677 the town had raised its proportion of the salary to twenty pounds.

In 1687 though the method of support was the same the salary of the master, not including tuition, was cut from thirty to twenty pounds and five pounds given to each of the two ends of the town for the instruction of the children in reading, writing, and ciphering.   This indicates a dissatisfaction on the part of the outlying districts with their opportunities for schooling.

In 1689 the master was paid twenty pounds and no mention is made of disbursement to the " ends."   Two years later the salary was made thirty pounds once more but " readers " were free and the school was held at three places in the town during the year.   This would seem to be a concession in order that the

---

[64] Ibid., 609.

community vote for the increase of the master's salary. By 1694, at least, the school had ceased to move and in 1695 the master taught a fixed school and received thirty pounds from the town together with the benefit of scholars. The following year the town voted to "give to him the said Mr. Nicholas Webster thirty pounds for one year in country pay provided he demand but four pence per weeke for Lattin schollers and teach all the Towns children that come to him to read write & cipher freely without pay."[65]

After 1697 there is no record indicating tuition charges; a moving school was established in 1702.

The town of Northampton in 1663 began the support of the town school by voting six pounds from the rates and whatever tuition charges might be collected from those attending school— this was to cover the cost for six months.[66] For the three years following there is no mention of a school, but in '66

"It was agreed and vote that William Jeanes was hired by the Towne to teach schoole one yeare, and for his encouragement and satisfaction for his attendance vpon that worke the Towne and himself came to this conclusion and Agreement.

1tly Impr for the yeare hee is to haue out of the Towne stock Tenn pounds wch the Townesmen promise to pay.

2ly ffowre pence pr weeke for such as are in the primer & other English bookes.

3. Six pence pr weeke to learne the Accidence wrighting Casting Accounts.

4. In case ther be a neglect yt they doe not come constant 3 days shalbe a counted as a weeke."[67]

In 1676 it was voted to "giue Mr. (Joseph) Hawly An Invitation to teach schole in his Towne on the same conditions or termes as formerly."[68] According to Hawley's account book these conditions were a fixed tuition charge per week and supply from the town instead of a fixed sum as agreed upon in '63 and '66. In '84 a similar agreement was entered upon with Hawley and with the same method of support.[69]

In 1693 it was voted "to giue forty pounds per yeer for A Schoolemaster that might be attained fit for that worke and the

[65] History of Newbury, Currier, 395–412.

[66] History of Northampton, 142.

[67] Ibid., 191.

[68] Ibid., 194.

[69] Ibid., 383.

aboue said sum of forty pounds they Agree to pay for one yeare
And the Scholers to go free."[70]  This measure met with considerable opposition and another town meeting was called to recon-
sider the matter.  The vote was again in favor of support by
general taxation and the time limit was made twenty years instead
of one year.[71]

Palmer was late in establishing a school.  In 1750 it was proposed to grant money for a school but the resolution was lost.
A similar motion was made the following year with the same result.  In 1752 it was voted to have the school kept in the four
quarters of the town; money for the support of the school to
be raised by rate and apportioned to each quarter.  This measure passed and annual grants are recorded from '52 on.[72]

The recorded action of the town of Plymouth during the 17th
century with respect to schools is very meager.  The first mention made of a schoolmaster occurs in 1670 when " John Morton
proffred to teach the children and youth of the town to Read
and write and Cast acounts on reasonable considerations."[73]  No
action was taken on the part of the town with respect to payment and it is quite probable that the school was maintained
wholly by tuition.

Not until 1693 is there another record pertaining to the school
at which time

"The Inhabitants of sd Towne voted that the Selectmen of sd Towne
should Indeavor to get a schoolmaster to teach Childerne to Reade and
write & the Inhabitants will take care to defray the Charge thereof."[74]

As it was the inhabitants who passed the measure and the inhabitants who agreed to defray the charge it is possible that the
schoolmaster, if secured, was supported by a general levy but
it can not be decided definitely.

In 1696 the town voted to have a moving school to be held
in the four quarters of the town and "Agred upon the Raising
of Money for the defrayinge the town Charges which is as fol-

---

[70] Ibid., 426.
[71] Ibid., 427.
[72] History of Palmer, 285–89.
[73] Records of the Town of Plymouth, Vol. I., 115.
[74] Ibid., 224.

loweth Imprimis for the scoolemaster 33-00-0."[75]   This, of course, means that the salary of the master was paid by the town.

In 1699 a change in method was made by the following action:

"Voted that the selectmen should take care to provide A schoole Master for the Town with all conveniant sped & should settle him as neere the senter of the Towne as may be with Conveniency & that every scollar that comes to wright or syfer or to learn latten shall pay 3 pence per week if to read only to pay 3 half pence per weke to be paid by their Masters or parents & what shall remain due to sd scole to be levied by Rate on the whole Inhabitants in there Just and Equal proportion."[76]

An item of 13 pounds in the list of town expenses for 1703 shows that the tuition and supply method still continued.[77]

In 1704

"Itt was votted by ye Inhabitants That there should be a Grammer Scole Master provided for ye use of ye Towne for ye yeare insuinge which shall be settled in the Senter of the Towne....votted That There shall be a Rate made upon ye Inhabitants of ye Towne to Defray ye Charge Thereof."[78]

As the town was poor and had been recently presented for want of a grammar school it is possible that the town could maintain a school in no other way at the time which may account for the change in method of support.

In the following year another plan was put in operation probably through the influence of some of the inhabitants living near the center of the town combined with the unwillingness of those who lived at a distance to pay full rate.

"And wheareas sundry of the Inhabitants have subscribed themselves To become bound to pay Twenty pounds per year Towards the support of a Schoole in ye town for the next 7 years ensuinge beginning in October next ensuinge this date provided that a scoole Master be provided & settled nere about or within 40 rod of the old meeting house in sd Town & that sd Town pay 20 pounds per yeare during sd time of 7 years & all children sent to sd school excepting ye shildren of sd subscribers yt is to become bound to pay ye 20 pounds as aforesd That lives within one mile of sd school shall pay 4 pence per week for latten writing or sifering & 2 pence per week for reading & all those yt are without ye bounds of one mile & within the bounds of two miles to pay 2 pence per week for latten writing or sifering & one peney for Reading Excepting the Children

---

[75] Ibid., 246.
[76] Ibid., 270.
[77] Ibid., 316.
[78] Ibid., 319.

of such as through poverty are rendered oncapable to pay theire Children to goe to school free and all without the bounds of two miles to Com free & all fines yt are by Law devoted towards the support of the scole & the money to paid by the week as aforsd to be improved towards paying ye Towns part of sd 20 pounds & ye subscribers to have noe benifit theby."[79]

At the expiration of the contract this method was continued for a further term of four years.[80]

In 1716 three schools were set up for the term of five years and supported by the rent of town lands, the income from lands sold or to be sold, and the remainder to be made up by taxing the inhabitants.[81] No further record of tuition charges appear after this time.

The first schoolmaster in the town of Salem began his duties in 1637; nothing is said concerning the method of payment and there is no further mention of school matters until 1644 when it was ordered

"That a note be published one the next lecture day that such as have children to be kept at school, would bring in their names and what they will give for one whole yeare and, also, that if any poore body hath children or a childe, to be put to schoole and not able to pay for their schooling, that the towne will pay it by a rate."

This put the support of the school on practically a tuition basis.

Not until 1670 is there any indication of a change in the method of support. In April of that year the selectmen were ordered by the town to provide a grammar schoolmaster and agree with him for his maintenance. By the terms of the agreement he was to have 20 pounds a year from the town " besides halfe pay for all scollers of the town and whole pay from strangers." This method continued in force to 1677 when it was voted by the town

"Yt Mr. Daniell Epps is called to bee a grammar schoolmaster for ye towne, soe long as hee shall continue and performe ye said place in ye towne prouided hee may haue wt shall bee annually allowed him, not by a towne rate, but in some other suteable way."

The " suteable way " decided upon was a tuition charge of 20 shillings per scholar and the remainder of the 60 pound salary to be made up by the town. This balance, however, was not

[79] Ibid., II., 2.

[80] Ibid., 72.

[81] Ibid., 169, 170.

raised by rate but taken from the rent of certain commons and islands.

This year, 1678, marks the beginning of a series of gifts to the Salem school by members of the Brown family. The income from these gifts, from the commons, and from islands belonging to the town was sufficient, with a moderate tuition charge, to maintain the school. The following is a sample of the income from the above sources for the year 1700:

| | |
|---|---|
| Interest on J. Brown's legacy of 50 pounds,.............. | 3—00—0 |
| Interest on Wm. Brown's legacy of 50 pounds............ | 3—00—0 |
| Ryall Side........................................... | 22— 5—6 |
| Baker's Island....................................... | 3—00—0 |
| Misery Islands....................................... | 3—00—0 |
| Beverly Ferry........................................ | 6—00—0 |
| Marblehead Ferry .................................... | 18—0 |
| | 41— 3—6 |

During the next thirty-five years 798 pounds were bequeathed by various persons to the use of the Salem schools and no town rate was levied from 1670 or a few years later until 1734. This rate was levied under pressure of an outlying district which wished to be set off from town in order that it might have power to raise money to support a school of its own. The town decided to "raise by a tax so much with the annual income, appropriated to the Grammar and Writing schools, as shall amount to 250 pounds, exclusive of the bequests of particular gentlemen, and that the middle precinct, Ryall Side and the Village shall draw from this sum according to their Province tax." Varying tuition rates made up the balance necessary to support the schools and during the period covered by this study the Salem schools were not entirely free as we understand the term.[82]

The first action in Springfield with respect to the school was taken in 1677 and was as follows:

"Further ye admittance & entertainment of Wm Maddison as a Schoolmaster was voted, he being to take three pence for those he teaches only to read English, & four pence P week for those he teaches to read & write, as also four pence for those he teaches only to write, & the Parents or persons are to allow no more; But the town for this year as a

---

[82] Annals of Salem, Felt, Vol. I., 426–452.

Encouragement to him in this work do agree & promise to alow him ye rent of ye Towne land in Chickuppi.''[83]

The following year a change was made from support by tuition and rent to tuition and supply by the following resolution:

"It was voted and concluded to give Mr Daniel Denton twenty pounds salary for his encouragement in the worke of a Schoolmaster for the present year he continuing in that worke ye term of a whole year or in case It should so fall out yt mr Denton attend not that worke the winter season, then the vote of the Inhabitants was to give him twelve pounds, & to allow him time to plant & dress two acres of Indian Corn, in case he cannot provide for it to be done for him for his money. In this worke ye Parents & Masters of such as send yr children or servants being to allow to ye Towne according to ye manner of their allowance to ye School-master the yeer past.''[84]

No record of change in method is found until 1692 when the town

"Voted and agreed that al Children fro five yers old to Ten yeers old Compleate shal be by their Parents Sent to Schoole, & if not their Parents shal Pay or be rated for al such Children to the Schoolmaster, as if such children were sent by yr Parents or master.''[85]

A change from tuition and rate to tuition and supply was made in '98. The town voted that "mr. Joseph Smith keep scoole till the 14th of January next ensuing and those scholers as have gone to him to scoole pay towards it and the rest the Towne pay."[86]

In 1706, without being authorized by the town, the Assessors raised a school rate on polls and estates "without Laying of. payment on the Scholars that come to schoole."[87] Eleven days after the Selectmen had notified the town of this action a meeting was called and it

"Was put to vote whether the Schoolmasters dues should be raised on the Towns Poles and Estates without Laying anything on the Scholars, & ye vote was for ye Negative. It being declared that the scholars paying three pence P weeke, the dues by reason of that way would be Sixteen pounds Sixteen shillings & Six pence & then it was put to vote that whether the sd 16–16–6 should be layed on the Scholars & the vote for the affirmative part. Then it was declared that the charge for school-

---

[83] First Century of the History of Springfield, Vol. I., 131.

[84] Ibid., 137.

[85] Ibid., Vol. II., 205.

[86] Ibid., 350.

[87] Ibid., 372.

ing besides the proportion for scholars and the rent of the school lands would be 10–18–6 & then it was put to vote whether to raise sd sum on the Towne yt is the Towns Poles & Estates & ye vote was for the affirmative."[88]

It is evident that there was a decided difference of opinion among the townsmen with respect to the above resolution and the following year the matter was presented to the Court of Quarter Sessions for a ruling. The statement to the Court was as follows:

"In as much as the Law of the Province obliges this Town to keep & maintain a Gramer School writing school and reading school & that the Schoolmaster be suitably Incouraged & paid by the Inhabitants of sd Town, Now for ye better support of ye sd School & Incouragement of Learning, It is agreed and voted that the Parents & Masters of every scholar going to sd School shal pay three pence P weeke in Town Pay, & for the enabling the Town to recover such dues for each scholar, It is agreed that the Schoolmaster that shall be hired from time to time shall keep an Exact account of the Time of each Scholar comeing to sd School, & leaving sd School, & upon demand of the Selectmen, such Schoolmaster shall deliver to sd Selectmen under his hand an account of the scholars as aforsd, and the Selectmen or the Assessors from time to time are hereby ordered and empowered to assess the sums upon the parents & Master of sd Scholars & to affixe or adde the sd sums to their Town rates that shall be granted from time to time by the Town, for assessing and raising such further sums for Completing the Schoolmasters ful dues that shall be due him, and it is further ordered and agreed that the Selectmen consider who are such children or scholars as to be priveleged, & that sd Selectmen do exempt their Parents & Masters from paying for such children going to schoole In whole or in part."[89]

Later in the month "the Justices of the Peace at sd sessions did determine the sd schoolmasters dues to be paid as the other Town charges are paid" i. e. by rate.[90] This decision was given in July. In February of the same year, 1707.

"It was voted to allow the schoolmaster mr David Parsons pay for three quarters of a yeer & wt the Townes Land fals short of satisfying Together with the scholars pay, that the same be assessed on the inhabitants."[91]

It is evident from this that the town did not abide by the decision of the Court and that the method outlined in the petition, tuition and supply, still continued in force.

---

[88] Ibid., 373.
[89] Ibid., 74.
[90] Ibid., 375.
[91] Ibid., 376.

By 1713 the minority opinion expressed six years previously became stronger and the Selectmen were ordered by the town to present to the General Court the following question: " whether the Charge Arising for the School be to be levied on ye Inhabitants as the Province Charge or whether a part on the schollers."[92] The decision is not recorded but from the following record, six months later, one may conclude that the decision was identical with that given by the inferior court some years before and that there was now a majority to enforce the new method. The record is:

"It was voted to Raise fourty pounds in Town pay for mr John Sherman for his keeping the school there was also granted Three pounds & Ten shillings for Danell Coolys Dauhter Keeping school There was also Granted ffiveteen pounds in money or Corne at money price for mr Nathanell Downing for his keeping school......"[93]

From this time on, yearly grants were made which show clearly that the schools were supported by general taxation.

The first school mentioned in the Tisbury Records is a moving school held at three different places but no record is made of the method of support.[94] The following year, 1738, the town

"Voted that ye sum of Sixty five pounds in Money of the old Tener be raised upon the ratable polls and Ratable Estates &c of ye Inhabitants of ye Town of Tisbury & Districts thereof and that a List thereof be made by the assessors or selectmen of Tisbury & Committed to the Constable or Collector of sd town with a warrant to collect the same."[95]

It is probable that the school was supported by general taxation during the previous year, if there was a school.

Pelham began with a moving school in 1746, the town enacting as follows:

"It was Voted that there be Thirty Six Pounds Raised to Pay a School Master for keeping School.

"Voted that there be a School in ye town ye Six Months Insuing.

"Voted that the School be kept Sixtmonths at the Meeting house & two months at Ephriam Cowans & two months at Alexander Cushings."[96]

The school continued to be supported by general taxation.

---

[92] Ibid., 391.

[93] Ibid., 392.

[94] Records of the Town of Tisbury, 101.

[95] Ibid., 106.

[96] History of Pelham, 224.

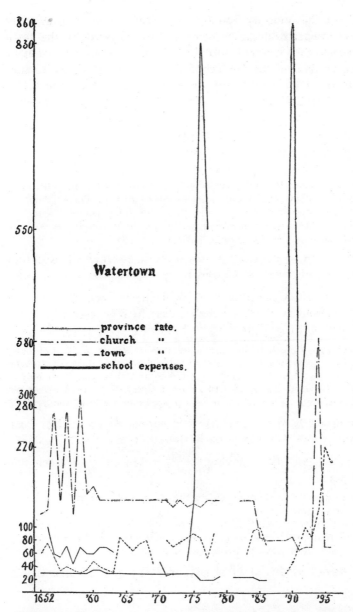

The record of church support .in Watertown begins with the payment of the
two pastors by rate and the building of a church to be paid for in three installments. Beginning with 1685 but one pastor was employed. Another church
was built in '94. Both war rates are here shown and at the time these rates
were levied we notice a decrease in the master's salary and a break in the con-
tinuity of the school.

The records of school matters in Watertown begin in 1649 with an order by the town for the building of a schoolhouse.[97] Three months later at a meeting of the selectmen it was

"agreed that John Sherman Shall wright a letter: in the Townes name: vnto Dauid Mechell of Stamfourth to Certify to him: the Townes desier of him; to come and keepe School in the towne."[98]

There is nothing in the records to indicate that a teacher was employed, however, until 1650; then at general town meeting,

"It was voted and agreed apon that Mr Rich: Norcrosse was Chosen Schoole master, for the teaching of Chilldren to Reed & write & soe much of Lattin, according to an Order of the Courtt, as allso if any of the sd towne, haue any maidens, yt haue a desire to learne to write yt the sd Richard should attend them for the Learning off them; as allso yt he teace such as desire to Cast accompt, and yt the towne did pmise to al-lowe the sd Rich; for his imployment thirty pounds for this yeare."[99]

On the next day, January 7, '50, at a meeting of the selectmen it was

"ordered, and agreed, that Mr Rich Norcrosse doth intend to begin his imployment for the teaching of the young ones of the towne and attend to it, at the meeting house the next day and further it is agreed, yt for his pay he is to haue it, at two seuerall times, the first at or apon the 29th of the 8th month −(51) and the other pay apon the 12th of the 11th month (51)."[100]

The allowance of thirty pounds on the part of the town was probably only in the nature of an agreement and did not signify that the amount was to be paid by rate. Mr. Norcross was an inhabitant of the town and as shown by the selectmen's record quoted above was expected to begin a few days after his engagement and teach during the year, yet in the list of town debts under date of January 19th, '51, the following item appears " Due to Mr. Norcros for his yeares seruice last past 12-00-0."[101] No other record of payment for the first year of service appears. It is quite probable that some system of tuition and supply similar or identical with that which went into effect January 12th, '51, was used during the previous year.

---

[97] Watertown Records, Vol. I., 18.

[98] Ibid., 18.

[99] Ibid., 21.

[100] Ibid., 22.

[101] Ibid., 28.

The agreement mentioned as taking effect in '51 is as follows:

"A General Towne meeting
An agreement Betwene the
Towne and mr Richard Norcros

That mr Richard Norcros shall attend the keeping of aschoole Within the Bounds of Wattertowne where the Towne shal appoynt, That he shall vse his best Indeauer to instruct all such psons as shall be sent vnto him in Inglish writeing or Latten according to the Capassity of the psons and that it is in the Li(berty) of any Inhabytant to send his sonnes or seruant for a weeke or two and to take them away again at his pleasure, and therefore the said Mr Norcros is to keepe a strict accounte of the nomber of weekes that euery one Dooth Continew, And that euery pson that learneth Inglish only shall pay 3d a weeke and such as write or Lattin shall pay 4d and that Mr Norcros is to giue notice to the pertickler parents of theyr Just Due according to this order and If any pson shall neglect to bring vnto his house his full due by the 29 of the 8th month in 52 that then he shall bring anote of the names and the sum of theyr debt vnto the 7 men who are hearby required to take some speedy Course to ( ) him to his due

And for the other halfe yeares pay hee is to take the same Course and what the ptickelers Doe want of the full som of 30 pounds the towne Dooth hearby ingage to make a supply."[102]

This method of tuition and supply continued in force until 1667 with an addition of 3 pounds as a gratuity to the master's salary in '53 " for those scollers that Com from other townes and the rest to return to the vse of the towne."[103] Mention is frequently made of tuition charges on children whose parents did not live in the town but it is not possible to trace the amount received from such sources.

As was mentioned above, the year 1667 marks another change in the method of support and for the first time the school is free to those who have " right and interest " in it. At the general town meeting it was agreed

"with Mr Norcross to keepe Schoole for the yeare ensuing: for 30 pounds: and the towne agreed that the Schoole should be Free to all the settled Inhabitanc: Children that thir Freinds liue in other townes; to pay as before; and their payment to be deducted out of the 30 pounds; and the remaynder to be made vp by Rate."[104]

As no special rate was levied for the school, the master being paid from the town rate in a lump sum, it is not possible to

---

[102] Ibid., 26.

[103] Ibid., 36.

[104] Ibid., 91.

tell how much the town realized from the charges on non-residents.

In November 1676, the town instructed the selectmen " to agree wth ascoole mastur as chepe as they can "[105] and in the following March an agreement was made with Lieut. Sherman to keep an English school for twenty pounds a year to be allowed him from the town rate.[106] In '79 Norcross was again hired at a salary of twenty-five pounds and both Latin and English were taught.[107] He was evidently succeeded after a year or so by some one who taught no Latin and thus the town incurred the displeasure of the Court for Norcross was hired again in '81 for twenty-five pounds with the " benifit of the latten schoolers over and above the said sum " as the parents of such children and Mr. Norcross might agree, and the " said Mr. Norcross doe Ingage to save ye Town harmless from fine: between this time and ye time of his beginning to keepe school: by teaching such latten schollers as shall be sent to his house."[108]

In 1686, Latin was again dropped from the course, the salary reduced to twenty pounds, and the tuition and supply method once more made the means of support. Recognizing that this method might make schooling impossible to some children who were able to attend when there was no tuition charge but would now be barred by the " 3 pens the week for Each Chilld " the town

"Voated Allso that the towne will pay for such Chilldren as thear parents are not abell to pay for The select men Being Judges of that mattur."[109]

No further records relating to the school appear until 1690 and, on the whole, there seems to be a growing lack of interest in school matters. Very likely there was little or no schooling during this period and the fear of the law was in the land. It was in this year voted that the town would have a school kept according to law and three men were appointed to make inquiry where a person might be found who could keep school.[110] This

[105] Ibid., 127.
[106] Ibid., 129.
[107] Ibid., 137.
[108] Ibid., Vol. II., 9.
[109] Ibid., 28.
[110] Ibid., 39, 40.

record is of interest also from another point of view as indicating the scarcity of men willing or able to teach. The committee was unsuccessful and later in the year the town offered fifteen pounds towards the master's salary, provided any of the public spirited inhabitants could agree with some schoolmaster who would keep a school which would satisfy the law.[111] The following January, about a month later, the following item appears:

"At ameting of the select men at Caleb Churches to meak the towne & Cuntry Reats At this meting the Cummitty sent Nathanel Stone about the Scoole mead thear Returne namely that thay had bene with him and had agreed with him to ceep the Scoole twenty parsons haueing ingaged to him to pay or se him payed ten pounds in mony yt is fifty shillings aquarter and allsoo the fiftene pounds granted by the town at the Jenarall town metting nouember 26–1690."[112]

There is no record of the town's paying the amount promised and it is quite probable that no school was kept. In November '92, mention is made of the town having been presented to the General Court;[113] and one year later the following agreement appears:

"At a mmeting of the select men then agreed with Mr Richard Norcros to kepe a grammer school for one yeare the yeare to begin the: 4 : of december next & to teach all such scollers as shall be sent to him to larne either to rede or wright prouided that the Parance or Masters of such Children to pay for theare teaching : inglish at : 3 : pence Per weeke & for wrighting : 4 : pence per weeke & for lattin : 6 : pence per weeke for each scoller & the scoll to be kept at his owne house vntill the first of aprill and then if vppon a monthes triall at the scollhouse theare apeare not a consederable quantety of scollers then he has liberty to kepe all the yeare at his owne house vntill the first of Aprill and then if vppon a monethes trial at the scollhouse theare not a considerable quantety of scollers then he has liberty to kepe all the yeare around at his owne house & the town to pay him : 5 Pounds in or as money besides each schollers proportion by the weeke but if he hath none but Latten schollers then mr Norcros to alow ought of his : 5 : pounds what such lattin schollers proportion cometh to: and if he findeth scholleres to come in to incurrage then he to keepe the scoll at the scollhous from the first of aprill vntill the first of october and the remainder of the reare at his owne hous and allso to caticise his schollers once a weke and all other Pirsons that are sent to him to be caticised."[114]

[111] Ibid., 42.
[112] Ibid., 43.
[113] Ibid., 54.
[114] Ibid., 62.

From fifteen pounds the town has now dropped to a contribution of but five; and there seems in the agreement to be a well defined feeling that not many children will take advantage of the school.

Again there is no mention of school activity until '96 when from fear of a fine the town was moved to action. At the December meeting, the selectmen reported to the town that

"they had treated with mer Edward Goddard on order: to his keeping a grammar scool as the Law directs: and his answer was that if the town would Repair the schoolhouse: and give him twenty pounds in money he would doe the best he could: but the town by a voate declared that they would not comply with mer Goddards proposals but by a voate Desired Corp John Page & Benja Gearfield to go to the nex quarter sessions to pray the Court that it is hopefull that the town will be prouided with a scool before the next quarter sessions."[115]

In February of the following year

"at a general town meeting it was put to uote whether the town would haue a gramer scool keept in the scool hous according to law and it passed in the negative."[116]

By the end of the week, however, the good citizens of Watertown were in a more law-abiding frame of mind and it was voted that the town pay ten pounds per year and the remainder of the master's salary to be made up by tuition.[117]

Finally in 1701,

"it was voted by the Inhabitants of Watertown at sd meeting that they will have a grammer school as the Law Requiers: and sd school to be keept the first qiarter of the year at the old school house: and the second quarter of the year in the middle part of the towne in such a place as the town shall appoint and the third quarter of the year at the old school house: and the fourth quarter of the year in such a place in the middle part: as the Inhabitants of the town shall appoint: 2: voted at sd meeting that the farmers precinct for the ministry: paying their proportion of twenty pounds with the town shall be freed from any further Charge referring to the school for this year: 3: it was voted by the Inhabitants at sd meeting that they doe desir mr Ames Angier; to keep the school as above said: and the selectmen are desiered & appointed to treat with mr Ames Angier for his acceptance of sd service and if mr Angier refuse to keep sd school: then the selectmen are desiered and appointed to procure some other meet person to keep sd school ;4; it

---

[115] Ibid., 109.
[116] Ibid., 110.
[117] Ibid., 110.

was voted by the Inhabitants that they doe grant a rate or tax: of thirty pounds in mony to pay mr Ames Angier or any other person that shall accept and perform sd service:'"[118]

Up to the close of the printed records in 1728 no change in the method of support by general taxation was made.

The following table is a general summary of the chapter.

| Town. | Settled or Incorporated. | First Rec. of Support. | Changes in Method of Support. | Moving or Divided School. |
|---|---|---|---|---|
| Boston | 1630 | 1636, **v. c** | 1644, r., t., inc. | |
| | | | 1650 r., ent. m. | |
| | | | 1751, rate. | |
| Braintree | 1634 | 1668, t., s., inc. | 1681, r., t., inc. | |
| | | | 1700, t., s., inc. | |
| | | | 1716, rate | 1716, d. s. |
| Brookline | 1705 | 1687, r., t. | 1704, rate. | |
| | | | 1705, r., t. | |
| | | | 1710, rate | 1710, m. s. |
| Cambridge | 1631 | 1638, t., c. | 1692, rate. | |
| Dedham | 1635 | 1644, c. | 1651, t., s. | |
| | | | 1685, r., t. | |
| | | | 1691, t., s. | |
| | | | 1694, rate | 1717, m. s. |
| Dorchester | 1623 | 1639, inc. | 1645, inc., c. | |
| | | | 1651, rate. | |
| Dudley | 1732 | 1739, rate | | 1739. d. s. |
| Duxbury | 1632 | 1734, rate | | 1740, m. s. |
| Fitchburg | 1764 | 1764, rate | | 1764, d. s. |
| Haverhill | 1645 | 1661, r., t. | 1673, t. | |
| | | | 1685, r., t. | |
| | | | 1712, rate | 1712, d. s. |
| Lunenburg | 1728 | 1732, rate | | 1733, m. s. |
| Malden | 1649 | 1701, rate | 1702, r., t. | 1701, m. s. |
| | | | 1710, t. | |
| | | | 1710, rate., | 1710, m. s. |
| Newbury | 1635 | 1639, t., c. | 1652, rate | 1687, d. s. |
| | | | 1676, r., t. | |
| | | | 1691, r., t. Eng. free 1691, m. s. | |
| | | | 1697, rate | 1702, m. s, |
| Northampton | 1654 | 1663, r., t. | 1676, t., s. | |
| | | | 1693, rate. | |
| Palmer | 1716 | 1752, rate | | 1752, m. s. |
| Pelham | 1738 | 1746, rate | | 1746, m. s. |
| Plymouth | 1620 | 1693, rate | 1699, t., s. | 1696, m. s. |
| | | | 1704, rate. | |
| | | | 1705, r., t., c. | |
| | | | 1716, rate | 1716, d. s. |

---

[118] Ibid., 140, 141.

| Town. | Settled or Incorporated. | First Rec. of Support. | Changes in Method of Support. | Moving or Divided School. |
|---|---|---|---|---|
| Salem......... | 1626...... | 1644, c., r...... | 1670, r., t. | |
| | | | 1677, inc., t. | |
| | | | 1734, inc., r., t.... | 1734, d.  s. |
| Springfield..... | 1636...... | 1677, t., inc.... | 1678, t., s. | |
| | | | 1706, r., t. | |
| | | | 1713, rate........ | 1713, d.  s. |
| Tisbury....... | 1669...... | 1737, rate............ | | 1737, m. s. |
| Watertown.... | 1630...... | 1650, t., s...... | 1667, rate. | |
| | | | 1681, r., t. | |
| | | | 1686, t., s. | |
| | | | 1690, r., c. | |
| | | | 1693, r., t. | |
| | | | 1701, rate........ | 1701, m. s. |

r—rate.
t—tuition.
inc—income.
c—contributions.
s—supply.

# CHAPTER V

## SCHOOL SUPPORT BY GENERAL TAXATION

Before taking up the Law of 1647, so well known in American Educational History, and which marks the next step in school legislation by the General Court, it may be well to bring together some of the more important conclusions which were arrived at in the previous chapters. We have found that the support of the poor in England passed through three stages: First the period of voluntary contribution, then of compulsory contribution, and lastly, the assessment of a general tax; that the last stage of this evolution in method was reached before the colonists came to America and hence would form a general background of experience which without doubt influenced them when meeting like problems in new conditions. We found evidence in the general sociological conditions, in the records, and in the Act of 1638 to justify the conclusion that the first and last stages were present in the development of the support of the town's poor in Massachusetts but, as might be expected, from familiarity with English methods the support of the poor became an item on the civil list some time before the like appearance of ministerial or school support.

We have shown the close connection between religion and education and presented evidence to show that the support of the church also passed through the contribution stages to practically unanimous support by taxation in 1660 and, because of this close connection, the inference is that the support of the church would influence the method of school support to a great degree.

Finally, the records show that, with respect to school support, the contribution stages were present in Boston, Charlestown, Dedham, Salem, and there is the highest probability that they were present elsewhere. It now remains to show the causes which lead up to the last stage—support by general taxation.

The Act passed by the Court in 1647 ordered

"that every township in this jurisdiction after the Lord hath increased them to the number of fifty house holders, shall then forthwith appoint one within their town to teach all such children as shall resort to him to write and read, whose wages shall be paid either by the parents or masters of such children, or by the inhabitants in general by way of supply, as the major part of those who order the prudentials of the town shall appoint; providing, those that send their children be not oppressed by paying much more than they can have them taught for in other towns; and it is forthwith ordered that where any town shall increase to the number of 100 families or householders, they shall set up a grammar school, the master thereof being able to instruct youth so far as they may be fitted for the university, provided that if any town neglect that performance hereof above one year, that every such town shall pay 5 pounds to the next school till they shall perform this order."[1]

In 1671 the fine was increased to 10, in 1683 to 20, and in 1712 to 30 pounds on every town of one hundred and fifty and 40 pounds on towns of two hundred families.

This law shows advance beyond the law of '42 in that it made schools compulsory and made the school a civil instead of a church institution. So far as support is concerned it contains nothing new but makes an application of the law of 1634 which made estates and abilities subject to rate for all public charges, and of the law of 1638 which made the inhabitants liable for all charges from which they might or did receive benefit. By authority of the first act a definite school rate, or money by way of supply might be levied on the inhabitants; under the second act tuition charges might be made upon all children of school age or on such children as attended school. These methods being authorized, various combinations of the above provisions were made as we found in the records and the summary following the preceding chapter.

The general tendency among the towns following the Act of '47 was to use a combination of the principles enunciated in, the Acts of '34 and '38 rather than to support the school entirely by rate or entirely by tuition. We find, however, that Boston began the support of its school, with the exception of entry money, by rate in 1650; Dorchester supported its school by rate in 1651, Newbury in 1652, and Watertown in 1667—thus following in principle the Act of '34. With the exception of Dorchester and Boston this method did not continue for a great length of time and was supplanted by some combination of tuition and rate. The method of support by rate being once used, the probable explanation of change lies in the objections of wealthy tax-payers; of those who, having no children in school, had little

---

[1] Mass. Col. Rec., II., 203.

or no interest in its support; and to the growing and general lack of interest in education.

There are several reasons why such a condition of affairs should have existed. As has been pointed out, the connection between education and religion in the early years was very close but it was not long before there was a decline in religious motives, due in great part to the large number of non-church members in the colony and the appearance of a new generation which was not actuated by the same motives and ideals as were the first settlers. Hence it was no longer the great concern of the inhabitants that youth should be raised up to the ministry; they became more and more engrossed with their own personal affairs and education did not seem at all necessary to further the clearing of the land or the planting of corn.

In 1675 the Indian wars began and a little later the expeditions against the French in Canada increased the burden of taxation enormously; this is shown clearly in the charts of expenditures for Dedham, Dorchester, and Watertown. Lack of interest and lack of money must have tended to reduce salaries, or decrease the length of school term, or both, and parents kept their children at home in many instances, without doubt, rather than pay the tuition charges. When the reaction set in and the Courts became more stringent and alert in presenting and fining towns, while at the same time the fines were increased, the above-mentioned conditions were of great importance in the forming of a new method of support.

Another factor to be considered is the settling of the more remote sections of the town, considering the church and the school as the center. Though the Court passed a law forbidding the erection of a dwelling house at a greater distance than one-half mile from the meeting-house,[2] in the course of time this restriction was necessarily disregarded as population increased. The farther removed the home from the center of the town, the more difficult it was for the children to attend school for the maintenance of which the father was taxed. Naturally he wished his children to derive some benefit from his share of the money paid for the support of the school and as the number of such parents swelled, their negative influence was strongly

---

[2] Mass. Col. Rec., I., 157, 181.

felt when the question of voting a town rate for the school
was presented. Those who sent children from a distance ob-
jected to paying as large tuition fees as those who lived near
by the school; probably some did not send their children at all,
and on all sides it became more difficult to raise the master's
salary.

Briefly, then, towards the close of the 17th century we have
a general lack of interest in education, more or less financial
depression, settlements being made farther and farther from the
center of the town, a loss of the communal spirit, laws making
schools obligatory, and a well defined tendency on the part of
those in authority to present and fine such towns as were delin-
quent in maintaining a school.

Let us trace the history of school support in a few of the
towns during the latter part of the 17th and the first of the 18th
century. The town of Haverhill in 1673 began the policy of
cutting down the town's contribution by rate to the support of
the school. This policy evidently continued for a long time and
from the fact that the town was presented during this time and
that records of school matters are very few, we may judge that
a method of support which did not include a general levy on
the town, was not conducive to the maintenance of a permanent
school. In 1711 the selectmen were directed to hire a master
who should keep school during the year in different parts of
the town. But when the selectmen found themselves unable to
hire a teacher under such conditions and suggested that a master
be hired to teach in the center of the town the townsmen refused
to vote a tax for the support of such a school. It seems reasonable to suppose, since the tax was voted when all the inhabitants
were to have the benefit of the school, that the second proposition was voted down by those who would not receive benefit of
the school when kept in the center of the town—aided by those
who had no children to send. In the following year the school
was divided and the rate granted.

The first school in Malden was not a town but a private school
which received now and then a small sum from the town as an
" incouragement " and incidentally enabled the town to avoid being
presented and fined. Evidently the school could not be kept up
by tuition and small encouragements from the town for in 1701
there is a record to the effect that the town was presented. The

town immediately voted a general levy to maintain a school in the four quarters of the town in succession, which gave all an equal opportunity to benefit thereby. In the following year there was a fixed school supported not by general taxation alone but by tuition and supply, thus throwing the burden of support on those who sent children to school, i. e., those living in the center of the town. This method was used until 1711 when the town decided to hire a master and dispense with the " supply." The town was presented within a month. Everything points to the fact that there was not a great degree of interest in the school but the law demanded that one be maintained. The evident price of its maintenance was the ability of all to participate in its benefits, for we find, as in 1702, that the general levy is granted in return for the moving school.

Plymouth in 1693 pledged the inhabitants to the support of a school; three years later the town voted for a moving school, thus indicating pressure on the part of those living at a distance for a share in the school if the rate for school support was to be voted. In '99 it was voted that a fixed school be maintained by tuition and supply. This method prevailed until 1716 when three schools were set up and supported once more by the general levy.

Watertown in 1676 was supporting its school by general taxation but at this time the town instructed the selectmen to hire as cheaply as possible. During the next four years, either because a school was not regularly maintained or because Latin was not taught, the town seems to have incurred the displeasure of the Court. In '86 the town levy was cut to twenty pounds and tuition was charged. In '90 the town offered to pay 15 pounds if some of the public spirited inhabitants would make up the balance sufficient to hire a teacher and thus satisfy the law. This scheme evidently did not work well for in '92 the town was again presented for want of a school. The following year the town voted to give the master 5 pounds and tuition, though it is evident from the record that it was not expected that many children would attend. Sometime between '93 and '96 the town was in trouble again with the Court. The town, having refused the offer of a master to teach for 20 pounds, sent a committee to the Court to inform that body that the town was expecting to secure a master soon. A master was hired for 10 pounds a year and tuition.  All this shows the lack of vital interest in education that has been previously mentioned and the failure of the methods of support indicated above to maintain a permanent school.  In 1701 the town voted to support the school by general taxation and hold it in two places during the year.  After this action there was no further trouble with the Court.

We see now from the records of these four towns, which are typical, what the effect of the lack of interest in education was— reduction of the town's contribution to the master's salary; a well defined tendency to place the burden of support on those who sent children to school; the consequent falling off in attendance; periods when no school was kept; and warning and fines by the Court.  In short, the method of tuition and supply had become inadequate to maintain a school.  On the other hand we have the absolute necessity of maintaining a school or being mulcted by the Court, and also a considerable number of inhabitants whose children could receive no benefit from a fixed school and who would therefore be decidedly in favor of allowing those who received the benefit of the school to support it or help to support it by payment of tuition.  It was out of these conditions that the moving, and the divided school took its rise.  The price which was paid for the voting of a general tax by which the school might be supported, beyond question, was, as we have seen, an opportunity for all the children of the town to attend school.  Hence it must move, be divided, or money must be given to remote sections that they might take care of themselves so far as securing a teacher for a short time during the year was concerned.  It will have been noticed in the account of the four towns given in this chapter that in every instance support by general taxation is accompanied by a resolution which does away with the fixed school.

Nothing can bring out more clearly the connection between support by general taxation and the direct participation of the outer sections in the town school than the following chart.  It will be noticed at the outset, 1691, that there is not the close relationship between such support and the rise of the curve indicating a general participation in school benefits as is shown some years later.  Take, for example, the year 1696.  The towns supporting their schools at this time by general taxation were Dorchester, Cambridge, Dedham, Newbury, Northampton, and

Plymouth. Dorchester, as we know, supported its school by rate from 1651—due no doubt to the influence of the law of '34 which gave power to tax estates for public charges. The town school of Cambridge did not begin until 1692. Because there was no hampering effect of custom, and because of the general attitude of the Court and the size of the fine which might be levied if a school were not maintained, the inhabitants were probably influenced to support the school by rate. The failure to maintain a private school by tuition and sundry encouragements from the town was probably the cause of the town school. No satisfactory explanation of the change of method in Dedham offers itse'f. We know that concessions to the more remote inhabitants were made in 1685 which continued in force until '91. From '91 to '94 these concessions were withdrawn and during the latter year support by taxation was voted. Whether this was a benefit to those who had formerly gained by the concessions of '85 or not seems impossible to determine; the moving school did not come until 1717. In Newbury the principle in question was active in 1687-8 and 1691-4. But after '97 all mention of tuition ceases though the moving school did not appear until 1702. Northampton presents another problem for which there is no definite solution at hand. It was a frontier town and therefore the settlers were not scattered to any extent; doubtless there was not much wealth and the major part of the inhabitants thought that support by general tax would bear less heavily on the community hence such a method was enacted though, as the records show, there was considerable opposition. But, in the large, the general parallelism of the two curves point directly to the one conclusion—the last stage in the evolution of school support, i. e., general taxation and the abolition of tuition charges, was due to the necessity of maintaining a school and the desire to have a fair return in schooling for money spent in its support.

This brings us to the last stage in the development of school support and also lays the foundation for our present system of free schools, that is, publicly controlled and publicly supported. The conditions which brought about the moving school established the free school and in the early history of the free school as a permanent institution, in the great majority of cases, it and the moving school were one.

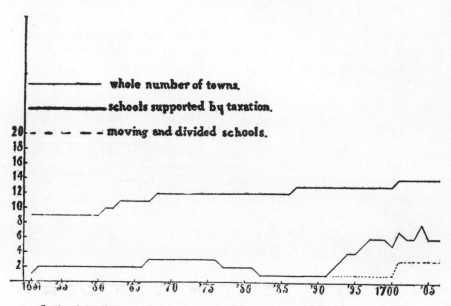

In the above chart the abscissas give the years and the ordinates the number of towns; The close connection between the voting of school support by general taxation is clearly of the period indicated by the chart. This is explained on the ground that such towns

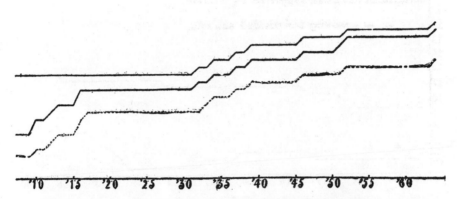

the data which forms the basis for the representation is found in Chapter IV.
shown, though there were towns which supported a fixed school by taxation at the close
were founded after the idea of school support by taxation had become general.

# CHAPTER VI

## THE " FREE SCHOOL "

The term " free school " was in common use in England for many years previous to the emigration of the Puritans, and, according to Leach in his work on the " English School at the Reformation," this term, various interpretations to the contrary notwithstanding, always meant freedom from tuition charges. The early colonial interpretation of the term indicates a similar meaning though some of the colonial " free schools " were not free in our understanding of what is meant by a free school, that is, a school supported and controlled by the public as a whole. A school which was free from tuition charges under any form of support through contribution could not be on a permanent basis and could not fill the conditions as stated in our definition of the term. The origin of the modern free school comes with the final step in the development of school support through the voluntary and the compulsory contribution, the combination of tuition and general taxation, and the conditions which caused the moving, or the divided school, that is, the origin and continued existence of the free school depended upon the opportunity for all to share in its benefits.

In his discussion of the " free school " Leach says that " it has been alleged that Free School did not mean free or gratuitous but (1) a Grammar School, (2) free from ecclesiastical jurisdiction, (3) giving a liberal education, (4) immediately dependent on the Crown, (5) free from the statute of mortmain. There may be other fanciful meanings devised to escape the obvious meaning. None of them can survive when confronted with the facts." He then shows at length that the term free school is applied not only to Grammar but to Song, and Writing Schools as well; that it could not have meant freedom from ecclesiastical jurisdiction for in every case the license of the ordinary was a necessity until within the last century; that it could not have meant that the Crown was the only authority for the statutes had to be approved by the Bishop and the master was almost invariably appointed by some person other than the Crown; that it did not mean a liberal education for in the schools founded in Yorkshire the word for liberal education is used and it is not *libera* but *liberalis;* that it did not mean free from the statute of mortmain for when such license was embodied it was a license to a limited amount only and the school was not freed from the statute generally. He concludes the discussion by saying,

"it is impossible that it could have meant anything but what it was popularly supposed to mean—free from the payment of tuition fees. Entrance fees, and all sorts of luxuries such as fires, lights, candles, stationary, whippings might have been paid for but free school meant undoubtedly a school in which because of the endowment, all, or some of the scholars, the poor or the inhabitants of the place, or a certain number, were freed from fees for teaching."[3]

Such are the conclusions of one who has made the most complete study of this question, and this must, of course, be taken into consideration when the term is used in the various Massachusetts towns. Yet this obvious meaning either entirely escaped or was only partly sensed by those writers on early education in Massachusetts who have attempted to define the term. Barnard writes as follows:

"The term was applied here, as well as in the early Acts of Virginia and other states, in the same sense, in which it was used in England, at the same and much earlier date, to characterize a Grammar School unrestricted as to a class of children or scholars specified in the instruments by which it was founded, and so supported as not to depend on the fluctuating attendance and tuition of scholars for the maintenance of the master."[4]

In an article on the first common schools of New England, Bush says,

"A free school—that is, a school for gratuitous instruction of poor children (as in this sense only were the early schools in this country free) can be traced back to the early ages of the Christian church."[5]

Brown, in his work on the Middle Schools, in speaking of Leach's study says:

"This is a clear and carefully guarded statement and seems to be borne out by the documentary evidence presented. It should be remembered, however, that in our colonial period, a'freeschool'was generally one in which school fees of one sort or another were regularly paid by

---

[3] Leach, English Schools at the Reformation, 110–114.
[4] Am. Journal of Ed., Vol. I., 300.
[5] Report of Com. of Ed., '96 and '97, Vol. II., 1168.

all but the poorest pupils; and was, moreover, a school of secondary grade, that is, a Latin grammar school.'''[6]

Bearing these conflicting interpretations in mind, let us examine the various instances in the town records where this term is used. Of the fourteen towns in whose records I find the term " free school " mentioned, twelve fall readily into one or the other of two classes, (1) the term used in connection with town action providing for the support of the master other than by tuition, and (2) the term used for the first time when change was made from support of the master by tuition and rate to support by general taxation.

Four towns fall in the first class. Boston in 1636, or at least the richer inhabitants, gave " toward the maintenance of a free schoolmaster for the youth with us " an amount a trifle over 40 pounds. Nowhere is there any information which would lead one to believe that tuition was charged. In 1682 the town took the following action,

"The same day it was voted by ye inhabitants yt the same Comittee with ye Select men consider of & pvide one or more Free Schooles for the teachings of Children to write & Cypher within this towne.''[7]

In 1686 we find the following record:

"And the standing charge of this town at this time is about 400 pounds ann—aboue 200 pounds of which is in maintaininge three Free Schooles, mending the highways in Bostone, Rumny Marsh, & Mudie River.''[8]

The inhabitants of Dedham in 1644

"did with vnanimous consent declare by voate their willingness to promote that worke promising to put too their hands to prouide maintainance for a Free Schoole in our said Towne
"And farther did resolute & consent testefyinge it by voate to rayse the some of Twenty pounds p annu: towards the maintaining of a schoole mr to keep a free Schoole in our said Towne."

It is difficult to determine whether this first school in Dedham was a Grammar School or not. Martin states that the " Dedham school furnished elementary instruction in English, writing, and the art of arithmetic "[9] but he does not give his authority for the statement. This would, of course, put the school out of

---

[6] Brown, The Making of Our Middle Schools, 32.
[7] Report of the Boston Rec. Com., Vol. XIV, 158.
[8] Ibid., 187.
[9] Martin: Evolution of the Mass. Public School System, 51.

secondary rank. Since there is no reference made in the records to the curriculum of the school until 1653, when the master " undertakes to teach to read English and the Accidence & to write & the knowledge & art of Arithmetick & the rules & practice thereof," one may infer something from the preceding teacher. Slafter states that the teacher for the first seven years was Ralph Wheelock, educated at Clare Hall, Cambridge University and took his degrees in 1626, and 1631.[10] With a teacher of such calibre it seems more than probable that the school was of secondary rank.

In the Dorchester Records for 1642 we find the following:

"It is hereby ordered and all the present Inhabitants of Dorchester aforsayd Whose named are heervnto subscribed" bequeathed and gave away their right and interest in Tomsons Island" for and Towards the maintenance of a free schoole in Dorchester aforsaid for the instructinge and Teching of Children and youth in good literature and Learninge."[11]

Again in 1655 we find the term used in the contract between the teacher and the selectmen:

"First that Icabod with the consent of his father shall from the : 7 : of March next ensueinge vnto the end of three full years from thence to be compleate and ended Instruct and teach in a free Schoole in Dorchester all such Children as by the Inhabitants shall be committed to his Care in Ennglish Latin and Greek......and also in writinge as hee shall be able."[12]

Then follows the clause in which the selectmen agree to pay the master to the amount of twenty-five pounds.

Roxbury in 1645 enacted as follows:

"Whereas, the Inhabitants of Roxbury, in consideration of their relligeous care of posteretie, have taken into consideration how necessarie the education of thiere children in Literature will be to fitt them for public service, both in Churche and Commonwealthe, in succedinge ages, They therefore unanimously have consentd and agreed to erect a free schoole in the said Towne of Roxburie, and to allow Twenty pounds per annum to the Schoolemaster, to bee raised out of the Messuages and part of the lands of the severall donors.

".......always provided that none of the Inhabitantes of the said Towne of Roxburie that shall not joyne in this act with the rest of the Donors shall have any further benefit thereby than other strangers shall have who are no Inhabitantes."[13]

[10] Slafter: The Schools and Teachers of Dedham, Mass., 8, 11.
[11] Dorchester Records, 104–5.
[12] Ibid., 73–4.
[13] Dillaway: Hist. of the Gr. School in Roxbury, 7–9, 30.

At the close of the contract made between the feofees and the master in 1668 follow the names of fifty-four persons whose children have right to the school and in a fourth column headed " gratis " are the names of four others indicating, of course, that the children of those families were to be taught free of charge.

In the second general division mentioned at the beginning of the chapter we have the following towns.

In the records for Charlestown for 1671 we find that the master was paid 30 pounds by the town and 20 shillings by each pupil. He taught them to read, write, cipher, and prepared such as wished for college.[14] Eight years later the following action was taken:

"It was put to vote to the Inhabitants of the town whether they would make a free school in this town by allowing fifty pounds per annum in or as money and a convenient house for the school master who is to teach Latin, writing, cyphering and to perfect children in reading English."[15]

Duxbury in 1741, when the change was made to a moving school, voted that while the schoolmaster kept school in the various quarters " that the school shall be a free school for the whole town, for any of the said inhabitants to send their children into any of the above-mentioned quarters where the school may be kept."[16]

In 1701 Malden under the proddings of the Court changed from the plan of encouraging a private school to a town school. The following excerpt from the recorded action is of interest to us:

"And he is to have ten pounds paid him by the town for his pains. The school js to be free for all ye Inhabitants of ye town......"[17]

Newbury in a similar change from private to town school enacted as follows:

"there was ordered and voted that the towne should by an equal proportion according to mens estates by way of rates pay foure and twenty pounds by the yeare to maintain a free school to be kept at the meeting house.  ..."

---

[14] Frothingham:   Hist. of Charlestown, 177.
[15] Ibid., 184.
[16] Duxbury Rec., 270.
[17] Corey:   History of Malden, 602.

The town of Northampton in 1693 changed the method of paying the master, and took upon itself the entire responsibility by voting

"to give forty pounds per year for A Schoole Master that might be attained fit for the worke and the aboue said sum of forty pounds they Agree to pay for one yeare And the Scholers to go free."[18]

Watertown voted in 1667 to support the master by general tax and " the town agreed that the Schoole should be Free to all the settled Inhabitanc: Children that thir friends liue in other towns to pay as before:"

Outside of these main divisions but bearing on the topic are the acts of two towns and a bequest made to the town of Salem. Ipswich in 1643 made provision for the education of seven free scholars but the school was not called a " free school " when this action was taken.[19]

Plymouth in determining the method of support and amount of tuition to charge for the various subjects in the curriculum excepted " the children of such as through poverty are rendered oncapable of pay." At no time was the school in Plymouth called a " free school."

In 1724, " Samuel Brown grants unto the Grammar school, in Salem, 120 pounds passable money to make the same a free school, or toward the educating of eight or ten poor scholars yearly."

Mr. Brown also made a bequest to the English school so that the income might be applied " toward making the same a free school or for learning six poor scholars."[20]

This completes the available data—let us see how well the definitions of the term previously quoted are borne out by the records. Mr. Barnard it will be recalled defined the " free school " as a Grammar School, endowed, unrestricted as to social class, and not dependent upon tuition.

But it is clear that the term was not restricted to Grammar Schools for in Boston writing schools were called " free schools;" in Salem the English school is called a " free school " in the bequest; and the " free schools " of Duxbury and Malden were elementary and not secondary schools.

---

[18] Trumbull: History of Northampton, Vol. I., 426.
[19] Waters: Ipswich in the Mass. Bay Colony, 146.
[20] Felt: Annals of Salem, Vol. I., 445.

The wording "specified in the instruments by which it was founded" indicates that an endowed school was meant for the ordinary church-town or town school had no instruments of foundation other than a town vote. Of all the schools mentioned but three were endowed at the dates given—Roxbury, Salem, and Dorchester. In 1648 Tomson's Island was taken from the town of Dorchester by the Court and yet we find the term used in '55. Roxbury, the best example of an endowed school, was a "free school" because of its endowment but it was not unrestricted as to class of children attending. School privileges were confined, in fact, to the children of subscribers and such poor children as the subscribers saw fit to admit.

Under the general educational conditions of the colony to have designated a school as a "free school" merely to indicate that it was open to all classes would have been a highly useless distinction. With the exception of the Roxbury Grammar School all the schools mentioned were town schools and controlled by the town directly or through the town's representatives, the selectmen, or through feofees elected by the town for the first few years of the school history as in Dorchester and in Dedham. The selectmen directly, and therefore the town indirectly, were held responsible for the education of all the children in the town by the Act of 1642; the Act of 1647 made the school compulsory. Under these conditions how could there have been any class distinctions with respect to schools which would have made the term "free school" of any meaning? Compulsory education and compulsory schools make such a reference totally beside the mark. And finally, the definition of a "free school" as given and the statement that this was the English meaning of the term is not upheld by Leach.

The definition given by Bush—a school which gave gratuitous instruction to poor children—has little or no support from the records. Plymouth and Ipswich gave such free instruction but the school was not called a "free school." In Brown's bequest to Salem he hopes to make a "free school" or, failing in that, to educate a number of poor children in which case we are to infer it would not be a "free school."

Neither does there seem sufficient basis for Brown's interpretation of the term. We find in all but two of the towns which established "free schools" that the amount of maintenance provided was equal to the salary of the master. This precludes the charging of fees, and no mention is made of poor children. The two towns mentioned are Boston and Dorchester; in the former the amount of contributions was but 10 pounds less than the master was receiving fourteen years afterwards, hence it seems probable that the master's salary was provided for without any supplement from tuition charges; and in Dorchester the intent, at least, was to make the rent of the Island cover the costs of the school. No mention is made of tuition charges in the lengthy and detailed school code and from the general disposition of the town towards school affairs which has already been stated at length it seems highly probable that tuition fees were not charged. That the " free school " was not always a Latin grammar school has been previously shown.

Other meanings than those given may be imagined but they as well as those given suffer the disadvantage of taking a decidedly less for the more obvious use of the term. On the basis of the records themselves we may assert that the primary meaning of the term " free school " as used in Massachusetts meant freedom from charge for being taught, and, as a corollary, schools were unrestricted as to whom should be taught except in Roxbury and in the case of non-residents. We have seen, too, from the records quoted in Chapter IV. that the free school except it was governed by the conditions imposed by the present conception of the term was not long in existence. The conditions which were fundamental to its permanency have already been stated in the conclusions of the preceding chapter.

In conclusion: We have shown that the support of the poor, and the support of the church before it reached the final stage of development—general taxation—passed through the preliminary stages of the voluntary and the compulsory contribution; we have shown the close connection between the school and the church; we have presented all that the records have to offer on the question of school support during the early period, and taking all the facts which bear directly and indirectly on the question, though not absolutely demonstrated it must be admitted that these facts point to the conclusion that town schools previous to 1647 were maintained by voluntary and by compulsory contributions.

We have shown that the law of 1642 made elementary education compulsory and—for the poor—made it free as well; that the cost of the education of such children was borne by the community. To what extent such free education of a few children in a community was influential in determining that all children be schooled at public expense cannot be definitely known, but with a growing spirit of democracy and its tendency to wipe out class distinctions it seems probable that this provision was a factor in the general line of experience which resulted in school support by general taxation.

And lastly, the records of the four towns, as examples, show that the method of tuition and supply or rate and tuition was not a method that would maintain a permanent school and avoid a fine which at the time seemed to be one of the highest educational motives. These records and the chart which follows show the closest of relationships between the maintenance of a school and the opportunity afforded all children to attend with least amount of inconvenience, and this maintenance was granted in the great majority of cases only on condition of equality of opportunity. This gave permanent basis for the free school—publicly controlled and publicly supported though the " free school ". had existed for a time much earlier but on a different basis of support.

# LIST OF REFERENCES CONSULTED

## Histories and Historical Essays—General

Byington, E. H.  The Puritan in England and New England.  Boston, 1897.

Campbell, Douglas.  The Puritan in Holland, England, add America.  New York, 1892.  2 v.

Doyle, John Andrew.  English Colonies in America.  New York, 1907 2 v.

Eggleston, Edward.  The Transit of Civilization.  New York, 1901.

Howard, George Elliott.  An Introduction to the Local Constitutional History of the United States, in the Johns Hopkins University Studies in Historical and Political Science, extra v. 4.  Baltimore, 1889.

Nichols, Sir George.  A History of the English Poor Law.  New York, 1898, 2 v.

Osgood, Herbert L.  The American Colonies in the Seventeenth Century,  New York, 1907, 3 v.

## Histories and Historical Essays—New England and Massachusetts

Douglas, Charles H. J.  Financial History of Massachusetts from the organization of the Massachusetts Bay Colony to the American Revolution, in Columbia University Studies in History, Economics, and Public Law, V. I., No. 4.  New York, 1892.

Ellis, George E.  Puritan Age and Rule in the Colony of Massachusetts Bay 1629–85.

Hutchinson, Thomas.  The History of Massachusetts from the first settlement thereof in 1628 until the year 1750.  Boston, 1795.  2 v.

Palfrey, John Gorham.  History of New England.  Boston, 1883, 5 v.

Weeden, William B.  Economic and Social History of New England, 1620–1789.  Boston, 1894, 2 v.

Winthrop, John.  The History of New England from 1630 to 1649, second edition, edited by James Savage.  Boston, 1853.

## Church Histories

Dexter, Henry Martin.  The Congregationalism of the last Three Hundred Years as Seen in its Literature.  New York, 1886.

Felt, Joseph B.  The Ecclesiastical History of New England.  Boston, 1855, 1862, 2 v.

Walker, Williston.  History of the Congregational Churches in the United States.  New York, 1894, 2 v.

### HISTORIES OF EDUCATION

Barnard. American Journal of Education, Vol. I.

Brown, Elmer Ellsworth. The Making of Our Middle Schools. New York, 1903.

Bush, George Gary. The First Common Schools of New England, in the report of the Commissioner of Education in the United States, 1896–1897, pp. 1165–1186.

Dexter, Edwin Grant. A History of Education in the United States. New York, 1904.

Dillaway, C. K. A History of the Grammar School or the "Free School of 1645 in Roxburie." Roxbury, 1860.

Leach, Arthur Francis. English Schools at the Reformation. Westminster, 1896.

Martin, George H. The Evolution of the Massachusetts Public School System. New York, 1894.

Monroe, Paul. History of Education. New York, 1905.

de Montmorency, J. E. G. The Progress of Education in England; a sketch of the development of English educational organization from early times to the year 1904. London, 1904.

de Montmorency, J. E. G. State Intervention in English Education; a short history from the earliest times. Cambridge, 1902.

Slafter, Carlos. The Schools and Teachers of Dedham Massachusetts. Dedham, 1905.

Suzzallo, Henry. The Rise of Local School Supervision in Massachusetts, in Teachers College Contributions to Education. New York, 1906.

Updegraff, Harlan. The Origin of the Moving School in Massachusetts, in Teachers College Contributions to Education. New York, 1908.

### RECORDS AND LAWS OF THE MASSACHUSETTS BAY COLONY

Shurtleff, Nathaniel B. (editor). Records of the governor and company of the Massachusetts Bay in New England. Boston, 1853–54, 5 v.

Whitmore, William H. (editor). The colonial laws of Massachusetts. Reprinted from the edition of 1660, with supplements to 1672, containing also the Body of Liberties of 1641. Boston, 1889.

Ames, Ellis, and Goodell, Abner Cheney (editors). Acts and Resolves of the Province of the Massachusetts Bay. Boston, 1869–1896, 8 v.

### LOCAL HISTORIES

Andover, Historical Sketches of. Sarah Loving Bailey. Boston, 1880.

Billerica, History of. Henry A. Hazen. Boston, 1883.

Cambridge, History of. Lucien R. Paige. Boston, 1877.

Charleston, History of. Richard Frothingham. Boston, 1845.

Dedham, History of. Erastus Worthington. Boston, 1827.

Fitchburg, Massachusetts, History of the town of, comprising also a history of Lunenberg from its first settlement to the year 1764. Fitchburg, 1865.

Hadley, History of. Sylvester Judd. Northampton, 1865.